8086/8088 Assembly
Language Programming

8086/8088 Assembly Language Programming

Bik Chung Yeung
Computer Training and Educational Centre, London

JOHN WILEY & SONS
Chichester · New York · Brisbane · Toronto · Singapore

Reprinted October 1985.
Reprinted November 1986.
Reprinted December 1988.

Library of Congress Cataloging in Publication Data:

Yeung, B. C. (Bik Chung)
  8086/8088 assembly language programming.

  Includes index.
1. Intel 8086 (Microprocessor)—Programming.
2. Intel 8088 (Microprocessor)—Programming.
3. Assembler language (Computer program language)
I. Title. QA76.8.I292Y48   1984   001.64'24   84-3618
ISBN 0 471 90463 5

British Library Cataloguing in Publication Data:

Yeung, Bik Chung
  8086/8088 assembly language programming.
  1. INTEL 8086 (Computer)—Programming
  2. INTEL 8088 (Computer)—Programming
  3. Assembler language (Computer program language)
  I. Title

  001.64'24   QA76.8.I292

  ISBN 0 471 90463 5

Typeset by Activity Limited, Salisbury, Wilts
Printed in Great Britain by
St Edmundsbury Press Limited, Bury St Edmunds, Suffolk

Contents

vi

Preface

This book is the result of a number of 8086/8088 assembly language courses given by the author. It is intended for the reader with some previous programming experience who wants to learn about the new 16-bit microprocessors.

Although the content of this book is based on the ACT Sirius computer, most of the chapters in assembly language programming are common to all 8086/8088 systems.

This book is divided into three main areas:

1. The hardware devices built around the 8086 processor.
2. The 8086/8088 instruction set.
3. Applications based on the ACT Sirius microcomputer.

Chapter 1 describes the 8086 family of devices as required by a system design engineer, and the internal structure of the 8086/8088 processor.

The Programmer's Tool Kit provided by the ACT for the MSDOS operating system is written for the assembly language programmer. Use of each of the programs is described in Chapter 2.

In Chapter 3, features such as the instruction format and some of the assembler directives are described, thus enabling simple assembly language programs to be written.

Chapters 4 to 11 explain each group of instructions with a number of simple examples. At the end of each topic, a practical example with solution is given.

Chapters 12 and 13 detail areas of the macro assembler, namely structure data type and macros. These simplify the task in low-level language programming once a large number of macros are set up.

The MSDOS operating system provides a user interface in assembly language programming. Both device and file handling are done through software interrupt. To explain this, a set of console interface routines are listed. A file DUMP utility program is also given as an example in Chapter 14.

Routines written in assembly language can also be accessed by high-level languages like PASCAL and BASIC. Chapter 15 shows the interface technique required for running programs under MSBASIC.

The ACT serial interface device provides the hardware required for intercomputer communications. An implementation of communication protocol for memory to memory file transfer with complete program listing is given in Chapter 16, and in Appendix C.

The ACT audio subsystem provides a means of generating sound and tone. Chapter 17 shows how one can initialize and program the system to produce an audio signal.

The ACT has a high resolution graphic display screen which can be used for curve and chart generation. The implementation of simple line and arc drawing algorithms is given in Chapter 18.

My thanks are due to many of my colleagues, friends, and students, in giving valuable suggestions during the preparation of this book. Special thanks are due to Mr G. Rowbotham, Mr. M. K. Gupta, and Mr R. A. J. Shah of International General Electric of New York, Radlett, Dr. J. Y. H. Au of Brunel University, and Mr M. Wu of STC, England.

My wife, Jennie, has not only typed the entire manuscript on an ACT wordprocessing system, but has also provided many of the original ideas. Without her definite support, this book would never have been completed.

B. C. YEUNG

Acknowledgments

My thanks are due to Mr R. Lee of the Computer Education and Training Centre, London, for permission to include teaching material from the course.

It is also my pleasure to acknowledge ACT (International) Limited for permission to reproduce a detailed description of the ACT Sirius computer, and especially to Mr J. Allason for his enormous amount of support and many communications.

I also like to thank Microsoft Ltd for permitting publication of details of the Software Tool Kit.

CHAPTER 1

Introduction

In 1978, the Intel Corporation of the US introduced the first high-performance 16-bit microprocessor, the 8086. It is only one of the CPUs in a family of hardware, software, and system support. In this chapter, each of the hardware components will be described. Section 1.3 describes details of the 8086/8088 CPU.

1.1   THE INTEL 86 FAMILY ARCHITECTURE

The Intel family consists of a number of hardware components:

8086	Microprocessor unit
8088	Microprocessor unit
8284	Clock generator
8282	Address latch
8286	Data transceiver
2716	ROM memory
2142	RAM memory
8205	Binary decoder
8255	Programmable peripheral interface
8259	Interrupt controller
8288	Bus controller
8089	I/O processor
8087	Numerical data processor

The 8086 microprocessor is a powerful 16-bit CPU packaged in a 40-pin configuration as shown in Figure 1.1. The 8088 microprocessor has attributes of both 8- and 16-bit microprocessors. It is directly compatible with the 8086 software and the Intel 8080/8085 hardware and peripherals. Both processors have a similar pin function description as shown in Figures 1.1 and 1.2 and Table 1.1.

1

2

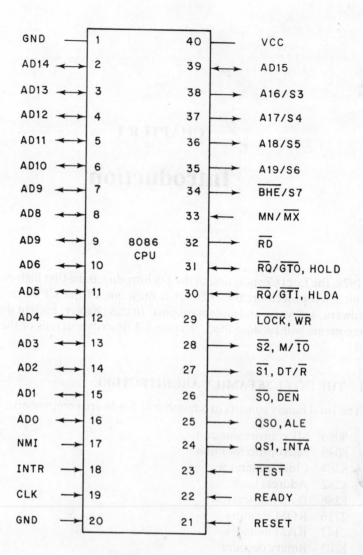

1.1 Intel 8086 microprocessor.

The Intel 8086 is available in three clock rates, 5, 8, and 10 MHz, while the 8088 can run at 5 and 8 MHz. This system clock can be driven by the clock generator 8284A/8284A–1 (10 MHz) using a crystal (Figure 1.3).

The 8086/8088 processor has a combined address and data bus commonly referred to as a time multiplexed bus (Figure 1.4). This technique makes the most efficient use of pins on the processor while permitting the use of a standard 40-lead package.

Each processor bus cycle consists of at least four clock cycles. These are referred to as T1, T2, T3, and T4. The address is emitted from the processor during T1 and data transfer occurs on the bus during T3 and T4.

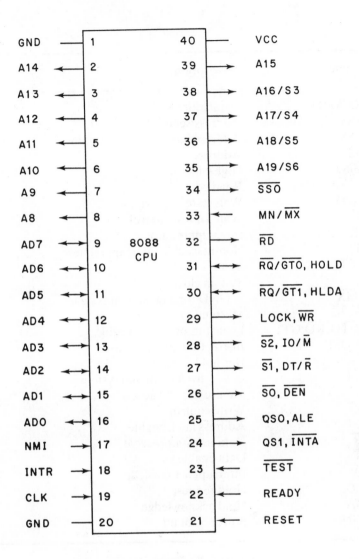

1.2 Intel 8088 microprocessor.

Using the 8282 octal latches with the strobe line (STB) connecting to the processors' address latch enable line (ALE), data (memory address) is latched into the latches during T1 (Figure 1.5).

The 8086 processor has a Bus High Enable line (BHE) to enable data onto the most significant half of the data bus to control the memory chip select function. This line should therefore be latched during T1 like an address line.

The 8286 is an 8-bit data amplifier that enables data to be transmitted and received in either direction (transceiver), with the Transmit line (T) and the Output Enable (OE) line controlling the data transfer direction. The 8086/8088

Table 1.1

Pin name	Description
ADO-AD15	Data/address bus
A16/S3, A17/S4	Address/segment identifier
A18/S5	Address/interrupt enable status
A19/S6	Address/status
$\overline{BHE}$/S7	High-older byte/status
$\overline{RD}$	Read control
READY	Wait state request
$\overline{TEST}$	Wait for test control
INTR	Interrupt request
NMI	Non-maskable interrupt request
RESET	System reset
CLK	System clock
MN/$\overline{MX}$	= GND for a maximum system
$\overline{S0},\overline{S1},\overline{S2}$	Machine cycle status
$\overline{RQ}/\overline{GT0},\overline{RQ}/GT1$	Local bus priority control
QSO,QS1	Instruction queue status
$\overline{LOCK}$	Bus hold control
MN/$\overline{MX}$	= V_{CC} for a minimum system
M/$\overline{10}$	Memory or I/O access
$\overline{WR}$	Write control
ALE	Address latch enable
DT/$\overline{R}$	Data transmit/receive
$\overline{DEN}$	Data enable
$\overline{INTA}$	Interrupt acknowledge
HOLD	Hold request
HLDA	Hold acknowledge
V_{CC}GND	Power, ground

processor provides the Data Transmit/Receive (DT/R) and the Data Enable (DEN) lines for this function (Figure 1.6).

Physically, the 8086 has a 20-bit address line that enables it to address 1 048 576 bytes (1 megabyte) of memory. Both random access memory (RAM) and read-only-memory (ROM) are required to complete a simple system configuration. Typical read-only-memory chips are the 2716 memory chip with 2K byte locations, and the 2142 RAM containing 1K × 4 bits each. A typical system configuration is shown in Figure 1.7.

The 8205 binary decoder and the 8255 programmable peripheral interface chip can be connected to the system to provide external device access. An output control signal (M/IO) from the processor is used to identify port address using the input/output instructions (Figure 1.8).

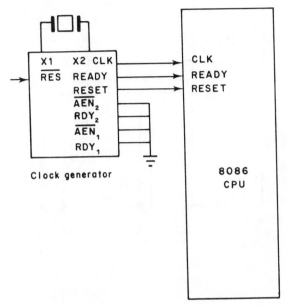

1.3 Intel 8284 clock generator.

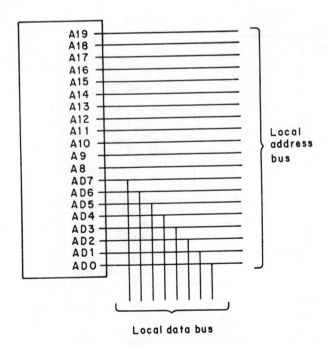

1.4 Shared address and data bus.

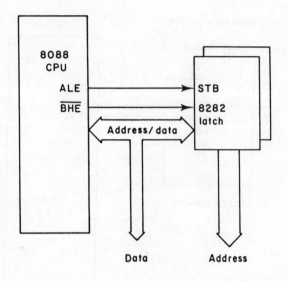

1.5 Intel 8282 latch.

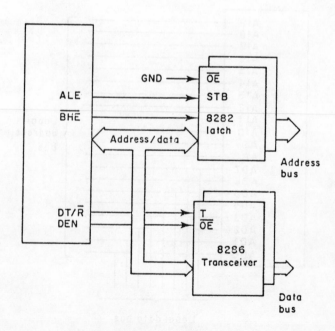

1.6 Intel 8286 transceiver.

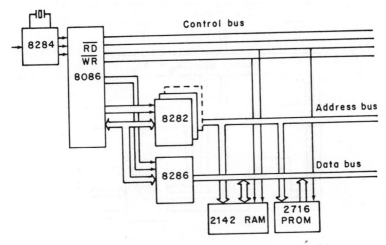

1.7 Typical system configuration.

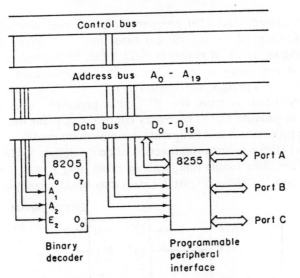

1.8 Minimum system with I/O mapped I/O port.

In small systems, it is simpler to reserve memory addresses for input or output ports, and then use the data transfer instruction to communicate with the device. Such a system is referred to as a memory-mapped I/O system (see Figure 1.9).

The most commonly used method of servicing the devices connected in this way is the polling approach, i.e. the processor tests each device in sequence and services the device when required. Thus a large amount of processing time is spent in the polling loop.

A more desirable method of servicing external devices would be to allow the processor to execute its main program and only stop to service the peripheral devices when it is needed. This method of interrupting the processor requires

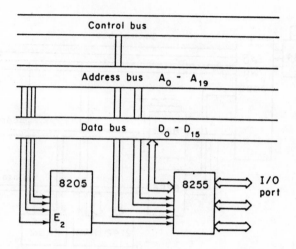

1.9 Minimum system with memory-mapped I/O port.

addition hardware. The 8259 programmable interrupt controller is a device specifically designed for use in real time, interrupt driven microcomputer systems (Figure 1.10). It manages eight levels of requests and has built-in features for expansion up to 64 levels. It is programmed by the system's software as an I/O peripheral (Figure 1.11).

For very large systems the 8086/8088 processor uses the 8288 bus controller to provide all the necessary control signals for the system (Figure 1.12). The processor is said to operate in a maximum mode.

The Intel 8089 performs the function of an intelligent DMA controller for the Intel 8086/8088 family and, with its processing power, can remove I/O overhead from the 86/88 (Figure 1.13). It may operate completely in parallel

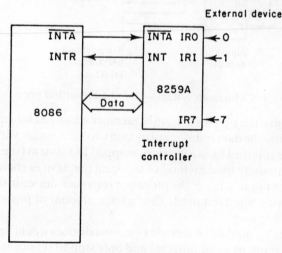

1.10 Intel 8259 interrupt arbitrator.

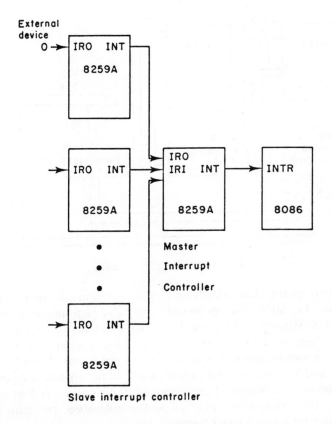

1.11 Multi-level interrupt.

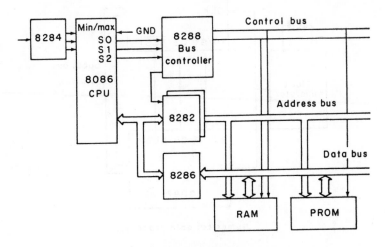

1.12 Intel 8288 bus controller.

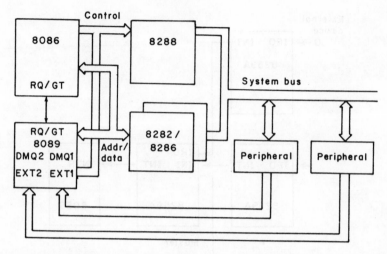

1.13 Intel 8089 I/O processor.

with a CPU, giving dramatically improved performance in I/O intensive applications. The 8089 provides two I/O channels, each supporting a transfer rate up to 1/25 Mbyte/sec at the standard clock frequency of 5 MHz.

The 8087 numeric data processor is designed for high performance numeric computing in conjunction with general purpose processing. The 8087 provides arithmetic and logical instruction for a variety of numeric data types. It also executes numerous built-in transcendental functions (e.g. logs and sine functions). The 8087, when attached to the 8086/8088, performs a useful range of operations much faster (Figure 1.14).

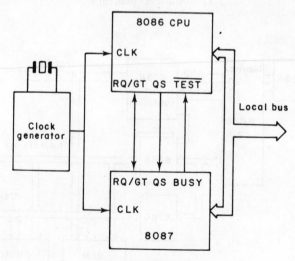

1.14 Intel 8087 numeric data processor.

1.2   ACT HARDWARE CONFIGURATION

The ACT Sirius 1 microcomputer has three modules:

1. The processor unit
2. The display unit
3. The keyboard unit

The Processor Unit

The processor unit physically supports the display unit, containing the main logic, disk drives, and power supply. The two integral single-sided 5 ¼ inch floppy disk drives store up to 1.2 megabytes of information. The system incorporates a minimum 128K bytes of random access memory (RAM), and can be expanded to 512K bytes.

The heart of the Sirius 1 processor unit is the Intel 8088 microprocessor. The main logic board consists of the central processor unit, the input/output section, the display section, the disk interface section, and the expansion bus (see Figure 1.15).

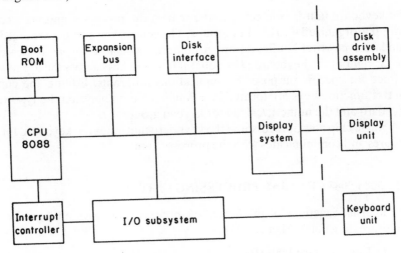

1.15 ACT block schematic.

When the 8088 is reset or powered on, the microprocessor goes to the highest memory area and begins to execute code in the boot ROM. The boot ROM software includes initialization of all hardware in the machine, and performs a cold boot from a disk which loads into the processor's system RAM the operating system software. When this process is completed, the boot ROM jumps into the operating system and begins executing.

Sirius 1 can be connected to a wide variety of peripherals and accommodates local and long distance communications. Standard interfaces include a parallel port (Centronic), programmable RS-232 channels, and an audio controller for digitized voice and tone output. All input/output ports are memory mapped.

The Display Unit

The display unit incorporates a 12-inch antiglare screen. It uses standard raster scanning techniques to display information on the screen. The most common mode of operation is the text mode, which displays 80 characters horizontally by 25 lines. There are five attribute codes associated with each character, i.e. reverse video, underline, high/low intensity, nondisplay, and user-defined.

A bit-mapped high-resolution mode is configured for 800 by 400 dots of bit-addressable display. In this mode, the reverse video, high/low intensity, and nondisplay attributes apply to fixed 16 by 16 dot cells on the screen, and the underline attribute is disabled.

The Keyboard Unit

The keyboard unit is connected to the rear of the processor unit via a coiled cord. It is organized into five key groups. The central key group is arranged in a standard typewriter configuration. A numeric/calculator keypad is located at the far right of the keyboard. The general function keys across the top row are defined for specific purposes by applications programs. Editing and cursor-control function keys are located in a double column between the typewriter keyboard and the numeric/calculator keypad groups.

A single chip microprocessor in the keyboard unit scans the keyboard for key closures and communicates with the processor unit.

1.3 8086/8088 CENTRAL PROCESSING UNIT

The internal functions of the 8086/8088 processor are divided logically into two processing units (Figure 1.16):

1. Bus Interface Unit (BIU)
2. Execution Unit (EU)

The bus interface unit provides the functions related to instruction fetching and queuing, operand access, and address relocation. This unit also provides the basic bus control. Up to six bytes of the instruction stream can be queued while waiting for decoding and execution. This queuing mechanism can reduce the 1.2 µs minimum instruction cycle to 400 ns and allows the BIU to keep the memory utilized very efficiently.

The execution unit receives pre-fetched instructions from the BIU queue, with memory operands. Results are passed to the BIU for memory storage.

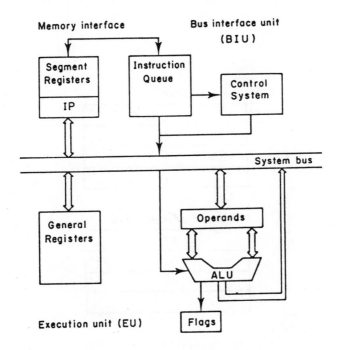

1.16 8086 CPU.

Registers

Comparing the internal registers of the 8086/8088 with the Intel 8080/8085, Figures 1.17 and 1.18 show that they are upgrade compatible.

There are 4 16-bit general purpose registers AX, BX, CX, and DX which can be used as 8 8-bit general purpose registers. These are used to hold intermediate results.

Apart from the stack pointer SP, there is one new base pointer BP and two index registers SI and DI. Pointers and index registers are for addressing specific portions of memory.

The instruction pointer IP is equivalent to the program counter in the 8-bit processor, and the flag register is also 16-bit with both status and control registers.

Segmentation

The processor has a 20 bit address to memory from location 00000h to 0fffffh. The memory is logically divided into four segments of up to 64K bytes each, with each segment falling on a 16-byte boundary (the last 4 bits of the 20-bit address must all be 0) (Figure 1.19).

General registers

-	A
H	L
B	C
D	E

Pointer and index registers

SP
-
-
-

Segment registers

-
-
-
-

Intruction pointer and flags

15						0

PC						
	-	S	Z	A	P	C

1.17 8080 registers.

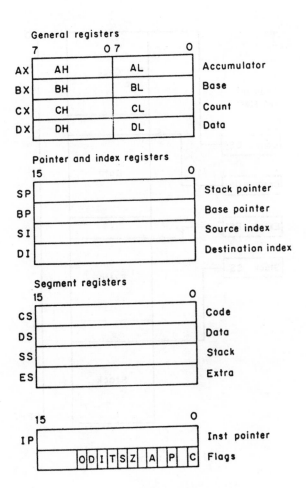

1.18 8086 registers.

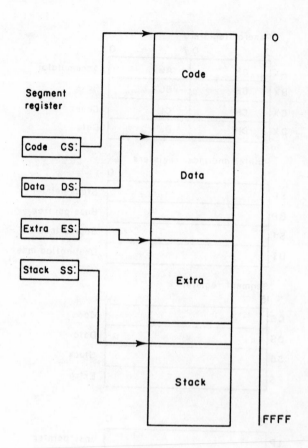

1.19 Segmentation.

A new class of registers, known as the segment registers, is therefore provided for memory addressing:

1. CS – Code segment register
2. DS – Data segment register
3. SS – Stack segment register
4. ES – Extra data segment register

Effective Memory Addressing

All memory references are made relative to a base address contained in one of the segment registers. This dynamic relocation scheme allows ease in segmentation of procedures and data for efficient memory utilization.

To calculate the absolute physical address, the contents of the 16-bit segment register have 4 zeros appended to the least significant bits, and the relative value (offset) is then added in the BIU to form the 20-bit memory address, offering 1 megabyte addressing range (Figure 1.20).

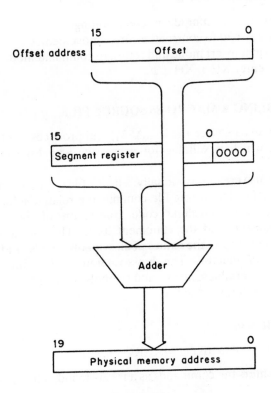

1.20 Effective memory address.

CHAPTER 2

MSDOS Programmer's Tool Kit

2.1 CREATING AN ASSEMBLER SOURCE FILE

PMATE is the screen editor provided for source editing under MSDOS.
To invoke PMATE, enter

PMATE ⟨filename.asm⟩ cr

Use ALT n to enter insert mode in screen editing.
Use the cursor key pad to control the cursor movement.
Type ALT x to exit insert mode and return to command mode.
To exit pmate, enter XE ± XH ±±.

2.2 ASSEMBLING A MACRO-86 SOURCE FILE

MACRO-86 reads a source file (__.ASM) and produces a relocatable object
file (__.OBJ), which is suitable for processing with Microsoft's MS-LINK
linker utility.

MACRO-86 also creates, optionally, a listing file (__.LST) and a cross-reference file (__.CRF). The listing file contains the relative address assigned to
each instruction, the machine code translation of each statement (in
hexadecimal values), and the statement itself. The listing also contains a
symbol table which shows the values of all symbols, labels, and variables, plus
the names of all macros. The cross-reference file contains a compact
representation of variables, labels, and symbols suitable for processing by the
MS-CREF cross-reference facility.

Invoking MACRO-86

There are two ways of invoking MACRO-86.

1. The user enters the commands as answers to individual prompts:

MACRO86 cr

18

2. The user enters all commands on the line used to invoke the assembler:

MACRO86 ⟨source⟩, ⟨object⟩, ⟨listing⟩, ⟨cross-ref⟩[/switch..]cr

Using method 1, responses are required to four text prompts (Table 2.1). When the last prompt has been answered, MACRO-86 begins assembly automatically without further command. When assembly is finished, MACRO-86 exists to the operating system. When the operating system prompt is displayed, MACRO-86 has finished successfully. If the assembly is unsuccessful, MACRO-86 returns the appropriate error message.

Table 2.1

Prompt	Responses
Source filename [.ASM]	enter filename to be assembled.
Object filename [source.OBJ]	enter filename for relocatable object code. (default: source-filename.OBJ)
Source listing [NUL.LST]	enter filename for listing file (default: no listing file)
Cross reference [NUL.CRF]	enter filename for cross-reference file, used with MS-CREF to create a cross-reference listing. (default: no x-reference file)

Command Characters

MACRO-86 provides two command characters:

1. Semicolon (;) followed immediately by a carriage return, at any time after responding to the first prompt to select default responses to the remaining prompts. This feature saves time and overrides the need to enter a series of carriage returns.
2. ALT-C at any time to abort the assembly.

Switches

Switches may be placed optionally following any of the response entries:

/D   Produce a listing on both assembler passes
/O   Show generated object code and offsets in octal
/X   Suppress the listing of false conditionals

2.3 CROSS-REFERENCE FACILITY

The MS-CREF cross-reference facility can aid the debugging of assembly language programs. MS-CREF produces an alphabetical listing of all the symbols in a special file produced by MACRO-86. With this listing, all occurrences of any symbol in the source program can be quickly located by line number.

Invoking MS-CREF

As with MACRO-86, MS-CREF may also be invoked in two ways.
1. The user enters the commands as answers to individual prompts:

   CREF cr

2. The user enters all commands on the line used to invoke the assembler:

   CREF ⟨crffile⟩, ⟨listing⟩cr

Using method 1, responses are required to two text prompts (Table 2.2).

Table 2.2

Prompt	Responses
Cross reference [.CRF]	enter filename to be used
Listing filename [source.REF]	enter filename for cross-reference listing. (default: crf-filename.REF)

2.4 MS-LINK

MS-LINK combines several object modules into one relocatable module (__.EXE). It also produces an optional list file (__.MAP) that shows external references resolved and any error message.

Invoking MS-LINK

There are three ways of invoking MS-LINK.
1. The user enters the commands as answers to individual prompts:

   LINK cr

2. The user enters all commands on the line used to invoke the assembler:

   LINK ⟨filenames⟩[/switches] cr

3. The user invokes MS-LINK with the name of a response file

   LINK %⟨filespec⟩ cr

Using method 1, responses are required to four text prompts (Table 2.3).

Table 2.3

Prompt	Responses
Object modules [.OBJ]:	enter filename to be linked, separated by blank spaces or plus signs (+). If plus sign is last character entered, prompt will re-appear.
Run file [Object-file.EXE]:	enter filename for executable binary code. (default: first object-filename.EXE)
List file [NUL.MAP]:	enter filename for listing file. (default: no listing file)
Libraries [NUL.LIB]:	enter filename for library modules to be searched. (default: no search)
Switches	
/DSALLOCATE	Load data at high end of data segment.
/HIGH	Place run file as high as possible in memory.
/LINENUMBERS	Include line number in list file.
/MAP	List all global symbols with definitions
/PAUSE	Halt linker session and wait for ⟨carriage return⟩ key.
/STACK:⟨number⟩	Set fixed stack size in run file.

In method 3, filespec is the name of a response file. A response file contains answers to the MS-LINK prompts.

Figure 2.1 shows an assembly language programming development cycle.

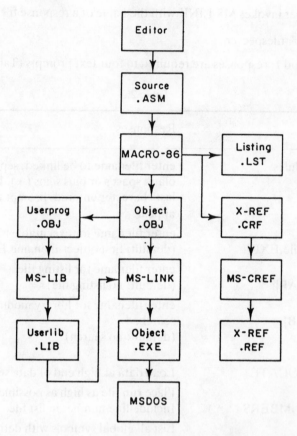

2.1 Assembly language programming development cycle.

2.5 DEBUG

DEBUG is a debugging program used to provide a controlled testing environment for an executable object file.

To invoke DEBUG, enter

DEBUG [filename]

where filename is the file to be debugged, and the ⟨arglist⟩ is the rest of the command line (Tables 2.4 and 2.5).

Table 2.4

Debug command	Function
D [⟨address⟩ [L⟨value⟩]] D [⟨range⟩]	Dump
E⟨address⟩ [⟨list⟩]	Enter
G[=⟨address⟩ [⟨address⟩ ...]]	Go
Q	Quit
R[⟨register-name⟩]	Register
T[=⟨address⟩] [⟨value⟩]	Trace
U[⟨address⟩ [L⟨value⟩] U[⟨range⟩]	Unassemble

Table 2.5

Parameter	Definition
⟨address⟩	A two-part hexadecimal number segment reg: offset segment address: offset
⟨byte⟩	A two-digit hexadecimal value
⟨drive⟩	A one-digit hexadecimal value 0=A:, 1=B:
⟨list⟩	A series of ⟨byte⟩ values
⟨range⟩	⟨address⟩ ⟨address⟩ ⟨address⟩ L ⟨value⟩
⟨record⟩	A 1 to 3 digit hexadecimal value used to indicate the logical record number on the disk
⟨value⟩	A hexadecimal value up to 4 digits

Example of a source file listing:

```
code    segment
        assume cs:code, ds:t__data, ss:stack
go:     mov  ax,t__data
        mov  ds,ax                ;load data segment address
        mov  ax,stack
        mov  ss,ax                ;load stack segment address
        mov  sp,offset top        ;load stack pointer
```

```
            mov    ax,nwd                ;load from memory
            mov    bx,ax                 ;move reg ax to bx
            mov    cx,bx                 ;move reg bx to cx
            mov    dx,cs                 ;move reg cx to dx
            int    23h                   ;return to op sys.
code        ends

t__data segment
nwd         dw     0ffffh                ;define, init variable
t__data ends

stack       segment    stack
            db         256 dup(?)
top         equ        $
stack       ends

            end go
```

For example, to use the above file for DEBUG, it is necessary to generate a .EXE file from the source file using MACRO-86 and the LINKER.

The .LST listing file and a typical screen dialogue is as follows:

```
0000                   code  segment
                             assume cs:code,ds:t__data,ss:stack
0000  B8 —— R    go: mov  ax,t__data
0003  8E D8          mov  ds,ax                  ;init ds to t__data
0005  B8 —— R        mov  ax,stack
0008  8E D0          mov  ss,ax                  ;init ss to stack
000A  BC 0100 R      mov  sp,offset s__data      ;set stack pointer

000D  A1 0000 R      mov  ax,nwd                 ;load from memory
0010  8B D8          mov  bx,ax                  ;move reg ax to bx
0012  8B CB          mov  cx,bx                  ;move reg bx to cx
0014  8B D1          mov  dx,cx                  ;move reg cx to dx

0016  CD 23          int   23h                   ;exit

0018                 code ends
                     ;
                     ;    data  segment
                     ;
0000                 t__data  segment
0000  FFFF           nwd      dw        0ffffh    ;init variable
0002                 t__data  ends
                     ;
                     ;           stack segment
                     ;
0000                 stack      segment   STACK
```

```
0000   0100 [                   db        256 dup(?)
              ??
                    ]
= 0100          s_data   equ      $
0100            stack    ends
                         end      go
```

Segments and groups:

Name	Size	align	combine class
CODE	0018	PARA	NONE
STACK	0100	PARA	STACK
T_DATA	0002	PARA	NONE

Symbols:

Name	Type	Value	Attr
GO	L NEAR	0000	CODE
NWD	L WORD	0000	T_DATA
S_DATA	Number	0100	STACK

Debug 86debug.exe

DEBUG-86 version 1.07

```
>u
0493:0000 B89504             MOV       AX,0495
0493:0003 8ED8               MOV       DS,AX
0493:0005 B88304             MOV       AX,0483
0493:0008 8ED0               MOV       SS,AX
0493:000A BC0001             MOV       SP,0100
0493:000D A10000             MOV       AX,[0000]
0493:0010 8BD8               MOV       BX,AX
0493:0012 8BCB               MOV       CX,BX
0493:0014 8BD1               MOV       DX,CX
0493:0016 CD23               INT       23
0493:0018 0000               ADD       [BX+SI],AL
0493:001A 0000               ADD       [BX+SI],AL
0493:001C 0000               ADD       [BX+SI],AL
0493:001E 0000               ADD       [BX+SI],AL
>t

AX=0495 BX=0000 CX=0278 DX=0000 SP=0100 BP=0000 SI=0000 DI=0000
DS=0473 ES=0473 SS=0483 CS=0493 IP=0003 NV UP DI PL NZ NA PO NC
```

```
0493:0003 8ED8                    MOV        DS,AX
>t

AX=0483 BX=0000 CX=0278 DX=0000 SP=0100 BP=0000 SI=0000 DI=0000
DS=0495 ES=0473 SS=0483 CS=0493 IP=0008 NV UP DI PL NZ NA PO NC
0493:0008 8EDO                    MOV        SS,AX
>t

AX=0483 BX=0000 CX=0278 DX=0000 SP=0100 BP=0000 SI=0000 DI=0000
DS=0495 ES=0473 SS=0483 CS=0493 IP=000D NV UP DI PL NZ NA PO NC
0493:000D A10000                  MOV        AX,[0000]
>t

AX=FFFF BX=0000 CX=0278 DX=0000 SP=0100 BP=0000 SI=0000 DI=0000
DS=0495 ES=0473 SS=0483 CS=0493 IP=0010 NV UP DI PL NZ NA PO NC
0493:0010 8BDB                    MOV        BX,AX
>t

AX=FFFF BX=FFFF CX=0278 DX=0000 SP=0100 BP=0000 SI=0000 DI=0000
DS=0495 ES=0473 SS=0483 CS=0493 IP=0012 NV UP DI PL NZ NA PO NC
0493:0012 8BCB                    MOV        CX,BX
>t

AX=FFFF BX=FFFF CX=FFFF DX=0000 SP=0100 BP=0000 SI=0000 DI=0000
DS=0495 ES=0473 SS=0483 CS=0493 IP=0014 NV UP DI PL NZ NA PO NC
0493:0014 8BD1                    MOV        DX,CX
>q
```

CHAPTER 3

MS-MACRO-86 Assembler

MACRO-86 is a powerful macro assembler for the 8086-based system under MSDOS.

MACRO-86 produces a relocatable object code which can then be linked using the MS-LINK linker utility to produce a relocatable executable object code. MACRO-86 is a two-pass assembler, which means that the source file is read twice. During the first pass, the assembler evaluates the statements, expands the macro call, and builds a symbol table where all symbols, variables, labels, and macros are assigned values. During the second pass, the assembler fills in the symbols, variables, and labels from the symbol table, and generates the relocatable binary file.

3.1 STATEMENT FORMAT

Each source statement is divided into four fields, which are separated by any number of spaces or tabs.

[Name   Operator   Operands   Comment]

Name –   The name field, when present is the first entry on the statement line, normally in column 1.

Operator –   Both 8086 mnemonic and assembler directives are supported.

Operands –   Each operand represents the source or destination of each operation. This could be a constant, a general register, or a memory address.

Comments –   Comments are preceded by a semicolon (;) and may appear by themselves or following each of the fields. They contain information which makes the program easier to understand but have no effect on the binary program they create.

27

3.2 NUMERIC NOTATION

All numeric values are decimal by default. This may be changed by the following methods:

1. .RADIX n
2. Special notation appended to a numeric value (Table 3.1).

Table 3.1

Radix	Range	Notation
Binary	0–1	B
Octal	0–7	Q or O
Decimal	0–9	D
Hexadecimal	0–9 A–F	H (first digit must be 0–9)

In .RADIX 16, it is necessary to have a leading zero for numbers beginning with A to F. A suffix H is also required for constants that end with B and D. For example, number 1B is not 27 decimal, but 1 binary (B), and 0D is 0 decimal (D).

3.3 NAMES

Names are symbolic representations of values. They are used in three situations:

1. Label – represents code
2. Variable – represents data
3. Symbol – represents constant

The legal characters for a name are:

A–Z 0–9 ? % _ $

Only the numerals (0–9) cannot appear as the first character of a name. Each name may be any length you choose, but must be unique to the first 31 characters.

A number of assembler directives are used to represent a name. Special names that are reserved for representation of 8086 registers must be avoided.

General Registers

The 8086/8088 has a set of eight 16-bit general registers. These registers are divided into two sets:

1. data registers
2. pointer and index registers

The data registers used in 16-bit operations are:

AX – Accumulator
BX – Base
CX – Count
DX – Data

and in 8-bit operations:

AH, AL, BH, BL, CH, CL, DH, DL.

The pointer and index registers are:

BP – Base pointer
SP – Stack pointer
SI – Source index
DI – Destination index

The Segment registers

The 8086/8088 is capable of addressing a megabyte of memory. This megabyte can be accessed through four segment registers by the CPU. Each segment can be up to 64K byte in size. The four segment registers are:

CS – Code segment
DS – Data segment
SS – Stack segment
ES – Extra segment

The four segments are functionally defined as containing code, data (DS, ES), and the stack.

Flags

The 8086/8088 contains nine 1-bit flags. They are divided into two types:

1. status flags
2. control flags

The status flags are:

1. CF – Carry flag
2. PF – Parity flag
3. AF – Auxiliary flag
4. ZF – Zero flag
5. SF – Sign flag
6. OF – Overflow flag

The control flags are:

1. DF – Direction flag
2. IF – Interrupt-enable flag
3. TF – Trap flag

3.4 ASSEMBLER DIRECTIVES

These are instructions which provide the assembler with the extra information required. These are divided into six different types:

1. Data definitions
2. Memory directives
3. Program linkage directives
4. Control of listings
5. Conditional assembly
6. Macros

The first four types are defined in this section, while conditional assembly and macros are explained in Chapter 13.

Data Definitions

There are 6 directives for data definition:

1. label – defines a name
2. define – reserves and initializes variables
3. equ – defines a symbolic constant
4. = – defines a symbol
5. record – defines a record
6. struc – defines a structure

Only the first four directives are described in this chapter, while record and struc are introduced in Chapter 12.

Label

⟨name⟩ label ⟨type⟩

By using 'label' to define a ⟨name⟩, you cause the assembler to associate the current segment offset with ⟨name⟩. ⟨name⟩ may be used for code or for data.

For code, ⟨type⟩ may be either near or far. A label defined as a 'near' type can normally be accessed within the same segment only, whereas the label that is declared as 'far' can be accessed from any other segments as well as from within the same segment. For example (Figure 3.1):

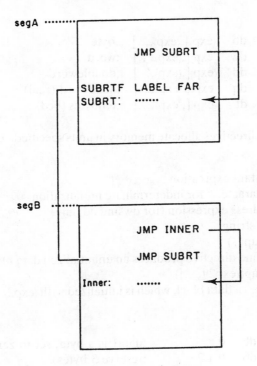

3.1 Example of LABEL references.

```
subrtf    label    far      ;define as a far label
subrt:    mov      ax,bx    ;define as a near label by (:)
```

The two labels subrtf and subrt both refer to the same address.

For data, ⟨type⟩ may be byte, word, dword, ⟨structure-name⟩, or ⟨record-name⟩:

```
barry    label    byte    ;define variable in byte mode
                          ;with no initial value
arry     label    word    ;define variable in word mode
                          ;with no initial value
```

Define

Variables are commonly referenced memory operands, each with a unique name in the program. Three attributes are stored when each new variable is defined, namely:

1. Segment – The segment in which the variable was defined
2. Offset – The offset (number of bytes from the beginning of the segment) of the variable defined
3. Type – The size of the data item in bytes

To define a variable with an initial value using one of the following DEFINE directives:

```
⟨variable⟩    db    ⟨exp⟩[,⟨exp⟩,...]    ;byte
⟨variable⟩    dw    ⟨exp⟩[,⟨exp⟩,...]    ;word
⟨variable⟩    dd    ⟨exp⟩[,⟨exp⟩,...]    ;doubleword
⟨variable⟩    dq    ⟨exp⟩[,⟨exp⟩,...]    ;quadword (real)
⟨variable⟩    dt    ⟨exp⟩[,⟨exp⟩,...]    ;tenbytes (bcd)
```

The DEFINE directives allocate memory in units specified. ⟨exp⟩ may be one of the following:

1. A constant expression
2. The character ? for indeterminate initialization
3. An address expression (for dw and dd only)
4. ASCII string
5. ⟨exp⟩ dup(?)
   the define directive produces an uninitialized data block
6. ⟨exp⟩ dup(⟨exp2⟩[,...])
   produces a data block which is initialized with ⟨exp2⟩

For example:

```
data1    db    0                          ;data1 is a byte, set to zero
datas    db    0,1,2                      ;reserve 3 bytes
                                          ;address by datas → 0
                                          ;datas+1 → 1
                                          ;datas+2 → 2
dataw    dw    ?                          ;dword is a word, no initialization
                                          ;equivalent to
                                          ;dataw label word
dataz    dw    0ff00h                     ;dataz → 00 (low order byte)
                                          ;dataz+1 → 0ff (high order byte)
dmess    db    'a string of characters',0
                                          ;define character string
                                          ;terminated with a null byte
darry    dw    20 dup(?)                  ;array of size 20 words
```

```
                              ;no initialization
dary2      dw    20 dup(0)    ;array of size 20 words
                              ;all init to zero
nptr       dw    go           ;near label pointer
                              ;1 word → offset of the label go
fptr       dd    far__go      ;far label pointer
                              ;1st word → offset of label far__go
                              ;2nd word → segment base value
```

where go and far__go are labels defined as near and far.

EQU

⟨name⟩   equ   ⟨exp⟩

Equ assigns the value of ⟨exp⟩ to ⟨name⟩. For example:

```
CR      equ    0dh
LF      equ    0ah
```

If you want to be able to redefine a ⟨name⟩ in your program, use the equal sign (=) directive instead. For example:

```
CR   =   0dh      ;carriage return
CR   =   0        ;current record
```

In general, symbols are declared in uppercase to distinguish from variables.

Memory Directives

1. proc   – defines procedure
2. segment – defines segment
3. group   – combines segments
4. assume – defines segment register content
5. org   – defines location counter
6. even   – causes the program counter to align with an even address

Proc

```
⟨procname⟩   proc   [near] .. default
                    or far

⟨procname⟩   endp
```

The 'proc' directive defines a section of code (procedure) that makes the programs more understandable. It can be executed either in-line, or as a branching instruction.

Segment

The segment/ends directive is used to define a logical unit called a segment. This segment may be combined with other segments in the same module and/or with segments defined in other modules. These segments will form the physical segments, located in memory, that are pointed to by the segment registers.

⟨segname⟩   segment [⟨align⟩][⟨combine⟩][⟨'class'⟩]

⟨segname⟩   ends

[align-type]   This field specifies on what type of boundary in memory the segment will be located:

page – Page alignment with address is xxx00H
para – Paragraph alignment with address is xxxx0H (default valve)
word – Word alignment with address is xxxxyH even address (y is even)
byte – place anywhere

where values of xxxx will be allocated by the linker.

[combine-type]   This field specifies how the segment will be combined with segments from other modules to form a single physical segment in the memory (Figure 3.2).

none – non-combinable (default).
public – all segments of the same name that are defined to be public will be combined (concatenated to form one physical segment up to 64K).
common – all segments of the same name that are defined to be common will be overlapped to occupy one physical segment; all of the combined segments begin at the same physical address. The length of the combined segment will be the length of the largest segment of that name.
stack – all segments of the same name that are defined to be stack will be treated the same as public.
memory – all segments of the same name that are defined to be memory will be combined so that the first memory segment encountered by the linker will be placed as the highest segment in the memory. Subsequent segments are treated the same as the COMMON segment.
AT expression – the segment is placed at the PARA address specified by the expression.

['classname']   The classname is used to indicate that segments are to be located near each other in the memory. Classnames must be enclosed in quotation marks.

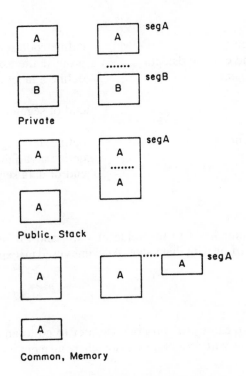

3.2 Segment combine types.

Group

name group segname[,...]

The group directive defines a group with the given name as a collection of the segname(s). The group directive is used by the linker to declare the segments that should be loaded together.

All segments in a group must fit into 64K bytes of memory. Once a groupname is defined, it can be used as any segmentname.

Assume

assume seg-reg:seg-name[,...]

or

assume nothing

The assume directive tells the assembler that the labels and variables in the segment or group can be accessed using this segment register. When the assembler encounters a variable, it automatically assembles the variable reference under the proper segment register.

The assume directive does not initialize the segment registers; each segment register must be initialized to point to the appropriate segments at run time.

For example:

code	segment	;define code segment go
	assume cs:code,ds:data	;promise the assembler
start	label near	;define a label
	......	
code	ends	;end of segment go
	......	
data	segment	;define data segment
date	db 1	;define a variable
data	ends	;end of data segment

Org

    org   ⟨exp⟩

The location counter is set to the value of ⟨exp⟩, and the assembler assigns generated code starting with that value. All names used in ⟨exp⟩ must be known on pass 1.

Even

    even

The 'even' directive causes the program counter to go to an even boundary. This is used specially with an 8086 processor where all memory access begins on an even boundary.

Program Linkage Directives

MACRO-86 supplies the necessary directives to support multimodular programs. A program may be composed of many individual modules that are separately assembled or compiled. Each module may define variables or labels that other modules may use.

Directives that are included in this group are:

1. name   – defines a module-name
2. end   – specifies the end of module
3. public – defines global names
4. extrn   – reference global names defines in another module
5. include – inserts alternative source file

Name

    name ⟨module-name⟩

⟨module-name⟩ must not be a reserved word. The module name is passed to MS-LINK, but otherwise has no significance for the assembler.

End

    end [⟨exp⟩]

The 'end' statement specifies the end of the program module. If ⟨exp⟩ is present, it is the starting address of the program. If several modules are to be linked, only one module may specify the start of the program.

Public

    public ⟨symbol⟩[,...]

Place a 'public' directive statement in any module that contains symbols you want to use in other modules without defining the symbol again. This information is passed to MS-LINK.

Extrn

    extrn ⟨name⟩:⟨type⟩[,...]

⟨name⟩ is a symbol that is defined in another module. ⟨name⟩ must have been declared public in the module where ⟨name⟩ is defined.

⟨type⟩

    1. byte, word, or dword
    2. near or far for labels or procedures
    3. abs for pure number

If the directive is given with a segment, the assembler assumes that the symbol is located within that segment. If the segment is not known, place the directive outside all segments.

Include

    include ⟨filename⟩

The 'include' directive inserts source code from an alternative assembly language source file into the current source file during assembly.

⟨filename⟩ is any valid file specification for the operating system. If the device designation is other than the default, the source filename specification must include it.

Nested includes are allowed. However, it is not recommended practice with small systems because of the amount of memory that may be required.

Control of Listings

Listing directives perform two general functions: format control and listing control:

    1. page   – set page size
                  start on a new output page
    2. title   – specifies a title
    3. subtitle – specifies a subtitle
    4. .list   – list all
    5. .xlist   – suppresses all listing
    6. %out   – output message on terminal

Page

    page [⟨length⟩][,⟨width⟩]
    page [+]

The PAGE directive with no argument or the [+] argument causes the assembler to start a new output page.

The PAGE directive with either the length or width argument does not start a new listing page.

⟨length⟩ page length in the range 10 to 255. The default page length is 50.
⟨width⟩ page width in the range 60 to 132. The default is 80.

The (+) sign increments the major page number and resets the minor page number to 1.

Title

    title   ⟨text⟩

The '*title*' directive specifies a title to be listed on the first line of each page. ⟨text⟩ may be up to 60 characters long.

Subtitle

    subttl ⟨text⟩

The 'subttl' directive specifies a subtitle to be listed in each page heading on the line after the title.

    Any number of subttls may be given in a program. To turn off subttl for part of the output, enter a subttl with a null string for text.

.List

    .list lists all lines with their code (the default condition).

.XList

    .xlist suppresses all listing. xlist overrides all other listing directives, except when another .list directive is encountered.

%Out

    %out ⟨text⟩

The ⟨text⟩ is listed on the terminal during assembly. %out is useful for displaying progress through a long assembly or for displaying the value of conditional assembly switches.

```
;
;              defining and initializing data
;
CR       equ       0dh                       ;carriage return
LF       equ       0ah                       ;line feed
FF       equ       0ch                       ;form feed
;
code     segment                             ;define test
         assume    cs:code                   ;code segment
         assume    ds:t_data                 ;data segment
         assume    ss:stack                  ;stack segment
;
exit     proc      near                      ;define a procedure
```

```
            int       23h                        ;return to msdos
exit        endp                                 ;end of this proc
;
go:         mov       ax,t__data
            mov       ds,ax                      ;init ds to t__data
            mov       ax,stack
            mov       ss,ax                      ;init ss to stack
            mov       sp,offset s__data          ;set stack pointer

            call      near ptr exit              ;return to msdos
;
code        ends                                 ;end of segment 'test'
;
;           data segment area
;
t__data     segment
;
;           define variables with constants
;
dbyte1      db        55h                        ;hex 55
dbyte2      db        101101b                    ;binary 101101
dbyte3      db        'test string'              ;ASCII chars enclosed in quotes
dbyte4      db        077q                       ;octal 77
;
;           define variables with types
;
dword       dw        0ffffh                     ;2 byte = 0ffffh
ddword      dd        0ffffffffh                 ;4 byte = 0ffffffffh
dqword      dq        ?                          ;8 byte with no initial value
dtword      dt        ?                          ;10 byte with no initial value
;
;           define variables with labels
;
nearptr     dw        near__label                ;pointer to a label defined as near
farptr      dd        far__label                 ;pointer to a label defined as far
;
darray      db        10 dup(0)                  ;initial 10 bytes = 0

t__data     ends
;
;           stack segment
;
stack       segment   stack
            db        256 dup(?)                 ;stack size = 256
s__data     equ       $                          ;top of stack
stack       ends
            end       go
```

CHAPTER 4

Data Manipulation

4.1 THE MOVE INSTRUCTION

The 8086/8088 assembler uses one instruction mov for moving data from one location to another. Operands can either be 8-bit or 16-bit in length, and they can be the general registers, any storage in memory, or an immediate data. The general form of the move instruction is:

    mov   des,src   ;move from src to des

Only the content of the destination operand is changed: status flags are not affected.

Operand Types

Registers

The 8086/8088 registers can be used as explicit operands to many instructions. In two-operand instructions, they may be used for both source and destination:

    mov   reg16,reg16   ;reg16 – 16-bit gen. register
    mov   sreg,reg16   ;sreg – segment register
    mov   reg16,sreg   ;
    mov   reg8,reg8   ;reg8 – 8-bit gen.register

Immediate Operands

The move instruction also allows constants to be specified in the source operand. Such a constant is known as an immediate operand, and can also be an expression that evaluates to a number. The move instruction is used to initialize registers and memory:

```
mov   reg16,imm16      ;imm16 – 16-bit immediate data
mov   mem16,imm16      ;mem16 – word mode memory location
mov   reg8,imm8        ;imm8 – 8-bit immediate data
mov   mem8,imm8        ;mem8 – byte mode memory location
```

Memory Operands

A memory operand refers to a particular location in the memory. The general term for a memory operand is an 'address expression'. An address expression may be a simple variable or label name, or it may involve registers, and/or constants. Each instruction can only have one memory operand:

```
mov   sreg,mem16       ;mem16 → sreg
mov   reg16,mem16      ;mem16 → reg16
mov   reg8,mem8        ;mem8 → reg8
mov   mem16,sreg       ;sreg → mem16
mov   mem16,reg16      ;reg16 → mem16
mov   mem8,reg8        ;reg8 → mem8
```

Memory Addressing Mode

The 8086/8088 has five different modes of specifying these addresses (Figure 4.1):

1. Direct addressing
2. Register indirect addressing
3. Base addressing
4. Index addressing
5. Based index addressing

Direct Addressing

The operand is a simple variable name. The name expresses the offset of the operand that is used to calculate the address. For example:

```
mov   ax,data          ;load ax with content of memory
                       ;specified by data → al
                       ;             data+1 → ah
                       ;with the data segment ds
mov   al,bytedata      ;load al with content of memory
                       ;specified by ds:bytedata
```

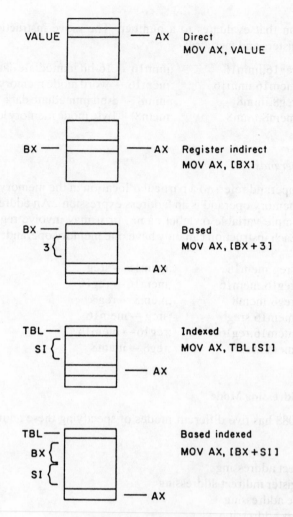

4.1 Data Addressing Modes.

Register Indirect Addressing

In this case, the offset of the memory is contained in one of the pointers or index registers (bx, bp, or si, di). To address the location you must first load the offset into the register and then use the register name in brackets as the operand. For example:

```
mov    bx,offset avar        ;load bx with address of avar
mov    ax,[bx]               ;load ax with content
                            ;specified by ds:bx → al
                            ;           ds:bx+1 → ah
```

Base Addressing

The base address mode is similar to register indirect mode except that a displacement value is added to the content of the register. With this mode, the register can point to the base of a data structure in memory and the displacement can then be used to access a field within the data structure. For example:

```
mov   bx,offset astruct      ;load bx with base address
mov   ax,[bx+5]              ;load ax with the content
                             ;specified by the content
                             ;of bx + 5, i.e.
                             ;the fifth byte of astruct
```

Base addressing is only used with either bx or bp as the base register.

Index Addressing

Index addressing uses si and di with a variable name to access data that is defined as array (see also Chapter 8). These registers are used as an index from the offset represented by the variable name. The contents of the register used as an index specify a byte displacement from the offset of the variable. For example:

```
mov   si,0                   ;set source index to 0
mov   di,0                   ;set destination index to 0
mov   ax,dsource[si]         ;load ax with 1st element of
                             ;dsource
mov   ddest[di],ax           ;store 1st element of ddest
                             ;with ax
```

Successive elements of the array are specified by offset 0,2,4,6,8..., therefore:

```
mov   si,6                   ;set source index to 6
mov   di,6                   ;set destination index to 6
mov   ax,dsource[si]         ;load ax with 4th element of
                             ;dsource
mov   ddest[di],ax           ;store 4th element of ddest
                             ;with ax
```

Based Index addressing

In this mode, there is a combination of both bx, bp, si, di, and an optional displacement. For example:

```
mov   si,0                   ;set index to 0
mov   bx,offset array        ;load bx with offset of array
mov   ax,[bx+si]             ;load ax with [bx]+[si]
```

The following two instructions are the same:

    mov   ax,[bx][si][2]

and

    mov   ax,[bx+si+2]

Unless a segment prefix operator is coded explicitly, the hardware defaults are as given in Table 4.1.

Table 4.1

Base/index register	Default segment register
BX	DS, data segment
SI,DI without a base register	DS
BP	SS, stack segment
SI,DI with a base register	that of the base register

For time-critical programs, Table 4.2 shows the added cycles needed for each addressing mode to access either 8-bit or 16-bit memory operands.

Table 4.2   Effective address calculation time.

Addressing mode	Additional cycle
Displacement only [disp]	6
Base or index only [BX],[BP],[SI],[DI]	5
Displacement + base or index [BX+disp],[BP+disp], [SI+disp],[DI+disp]	9
Base + index [BP+DI],[BX+SI] [BP+SI],[BX+DI]	7 8
Displacement + base + index [BP+DI+disp],[BX+SI+disp] [BP+SI+disp],[BX+DI+disp]	11 12

Attribute Operators

With each memory operand, it is sometimes necessary to override the segment, offset, or type of the variables in order to use them more efficiently. The assembly language provides attribute operators that can be used to:

1. Override (alter for one instruction) an operand's attribute
2. Yield the value of the operand attributes

Attribute Overriding Operators

Although the attributes of a variable are normally assumed to be its defined values, they can be overridden by the following attribute overriding operators:

1. Segment override
2. Type override

Segment override

    sreg:name
    segname:name
    groupname:name

The colon (:) operator overrides the assumed segment of an address expression for the current operand. For example:

    mov   ax,es:aword   ;load aword
    mov   ax,es:[bx]   ;override default seg-reg

Type override

PTR operator – the pointer operator

    ⟨type⟩   ptr   ⟨name⟩

The PTR operator overrides the type (byte, word, dword...). For example, to access just the lower byte of BDEF:

    bdef   dw   0ff0H   ;define bdef
            mov   al,byte ptr bdef ;to access data that is
                                     ;defined NOT as a byte

and to access the high-order byte:

            mov   ah,byte ptr bedf+1 ;high-order byte → ah

Value Returning Operators

These operators return the attribute values of the operands that follow them but do not override the attribute:

    1. seg – return the segement base address
    2. offset – return the offset value
    3. type, length, and size – return the memory allocation

Seg

    seg   ⟨name⟩

seg returns the segment value (segment base address) of the segment enclosing the label or variable. For example:

mov	ax,seg var	;ax ← segment base of var
mov	ds,ax	;setup data segment

Offset

    offset ⟨name⟩

offset returns the offset value of the variable or label within its segments (the number of bytes between the segment base address and the address where the label or variable is defined). For example:

mov	bx,offset var	;load bx with offset address of var
mov	ax,[bx]	;load content of var in ax
mov	bx,offset lab	;load bx with offset address of lab
mov	dx,[bx]	;load content of lab in dx

Type

    type   ⟨variable⟩
    type   ⟨label⟩

If the operand is a label, the type operator returns near (0ffffh) or far (0fffeh). If the operand is a variable, the type operator returns a value equal to the number of bytes of the variable type, as follows:

byte	=	1
word	=	2
dword	=	4
qword	=	8
tbyte	=	10

For example:

```
        mov   ax,type var      ;mov 4 in ax
   var  dd    0
```

Length

```
   length     ⟨variable⟩
```

length returns the number of type units (byte, word, dword etc.) allocated for that variable. For example:

```
           mov   cx,length array    ;get number of elements
                                     ;in array
   array   dw    100 dup(?)          ;cx = 100
           mov   cx,length ary2
   ary2    dd    0                   ;cx = 1
```

Size

```
      size ⟨variable⟩
```

size returns the total number of bytes allocated for a variable, i.e. size = length * type. For example:

```
      mov   dx,size array       ;length = 100, type = 2
                                 ;size = 100 * 2
                                 ;dx ← 200
   array    dw    100 dup(?)
```

As an example of the move instructions with different operand modes, 86move.asm is a listing of a complete 8086 program. The result of each instruction can be examined under debug. The label exit is defined as far in

```
   extrn     exit:far
```

This refers to a procedure that returns to the operating system level, and is defined elsewhere in chapters related to the two operating systems currently available.

To use a procedure, the instruction 'call label' must be used. A detailed explanation of procedures can be found in Chapter 10.

```
;
;       MOVE INSTRUCTION
;
        extrn  exit:far                ;external proc to return to msdos
code  segment                          ;name of this segment
        assume cs:code,ds:t__data,ss:stack    ;segment assignment
;
;       main module begin from loc go
;
;       init segment registers
;
go:   mov   ax,t__data                 ;address of t__data → ax
      mov   ds,ax                      ;init data segment to t__data
      mov   ax,stack                   ;address of stack → ax
      mov   ss,ax                      ;init stack segment to stack
      mov   sp,offset s__data          ;set stack pointer
;
;       move immediate data to reg
;
      mov   ax,0ffffh                  ;16-bit data 0ffffh→16-bit reg.
      mov   bl,'0'                     ;8-bit ascii'0'→8-bit reg.
;
;       move reg to reg
;
;       16-bit
;
      mov   bx,ax                      ;content of 16-bit reg ax → bx
      mov   cx,bx                      ;content of 16-bit reg bx → cx
      mov   dx,cx                      ;content of 16-bit reg cx → dx
;
;       8-bit
;
      mov   al,0                       ;immediate data 0 → 8 bit reg al
      mov   bl,al                      ;content of 8-bit reg al → bl
      mov   cl,bl                      ;content of 8-bit reg bl → cl
      mov   dl,cl                      ;content of 8-bit reg cl → dl
;
;       move reg/memory
;
      mov   ax,nwd                     ;content of the loc nwd → ax
      mov   dl,byte ptr nwd2           ;content of the 1st byte of nwd2 → dl
;
;       move memory with indirect addressing
;
      mov   bx,offset nbyte1           ;offset address of nbyte1 → bx
      mov   al,[bx]                    ;loc content specified by bx → ax
```

```
;
;       move memory/memory — must use a register in two steps
;

        mov     ax,nwd              ;content of nwd → ax
        mov     nwd2,ax             ;content of ax → nwd2
;
;       size operator
;

        mov     cx,size nwd         ;size of nwd → cx (cx = 2)
;
;       return to MSDOS
;

        call    exit                ;execute procedure
code ends                           ;end of this segment
;
;       DATA SEGMENT
;
t__data   segment
nwd       dw      0ffffh            ;define word with content 0ffffh
nwd2      dw      0f0fh             ;define word with content 0f0fh
nbyte1    dw      55h               ;define word with content 55h
t__data   ends                      ;end of this segment
;
;       STACK SEGMENT
;
stack     segment  stack
          db      256   dup(?)      ;define stack space
s__data   equ     $                 ;define top of stack
stack     ends                      ;end of this segment
          end     go                ;end of this program
```

4.2 EXCHANGE INSTRUCTION

The two operands are exchanged. Segment registers are not legal operands.

```
        xchg    reg8,reg8           ;reg8 ↔ reg8
        xchg    mem8,reg8           ;mem8 ↔ reg8
        xchg    reg16,reg16         ;reg16 ↔ reg16
        xchg    mem16,reg16         ;mem16 ↔ reg16
```

For example:

```
        xchg    bl,cl               ;exchange bl and cl
```

4.3 LOAD ADDRESS INSTRUCTIONS

There are four instructions for loading the address of a ⟨name⟩.

    1. mov   ;use OFFSET operator
    2. lea   ;load effective address
    3. lds   ;load pointer to register + DS
    4. les   ;load pointer to register + ES

LEA

The effective address of the memory operand is put in the specified register. This instruction is more powerful than

    mov   bx,offset name

because an index and/or a base register can be used to form the effective address:

    lea   reg,⟨name⟩

    mov   ax,offset name   ;load ax with eff. address of name
    lea   ax,name   ;is the same

where

    mov   ax,offset table[si]   ;is an invalid instruction
    lea   ax,table[si]   ;load address of table+si

LDS/LES

    lds,   les load pointer to ds/es and register, i.e.

        lds   reg,⟨dwordpointer⟩
        les   reg,⟨dwordpointer⟩

That is

    reg   = EA, EA+1
    ds/es = EA+2, EA+3

For example, to load the effective address of a variable that is defined in another segment in the base register, one can use the value returning operators, such as

    mov   bx,offset val
    mov   ds,seg val

or define a double word pointer and use the LDS instruction.

Each pointer defined by a dd directive sets the content of the pointer, and pointer+1, to the offset value of the variable name, and pointer+2 and pointer to the segment base value of the variable.

```
eptr      dd  evalue          ;declare eptr
evalue    db  o               ;declare evalue

eptr,   eptr+1=  offset of evalue
eptr+2,   eptr+3  =  segment base of evalue
```

and

```
lds  bx,eptr     ;load ds = segment base value of evalue
                 ;bx = offset of evalue
```

4.4 ACT SCREEN FORMAT

The Sirius display hardware is a memory-mapped raster scan system. The contents of the screen are stored in memory as a sequence of 80*25 words starting from location f0000h occupying 4K bytes. Each character is 10 dots wide by 16 lines high, which are RAM-mapped and programmable. With a data segment register ES = f000h, the character at the top left-hand corner has an offset of 0 and 1. Other offsets can be calculated as:

$$offset = y*160 + x*2$$

where y is the row number $0 < y < 24$ and x is the column number $0 < x < 79$.

Each character is defined in two bytes, the character offset in the font table and the attribute values.

The character offset in the font table is defined as its ASCII value plus 100 decimal.

The attribute byte is defined as

```
bit  0     inverse video
     1     half intensity
     2     underline
     3     nondisplay
     4     reserved
   5–15    font cell pointer
```

Being a memory-mapped I/O device, only the MOV instruction is required to output characters directly on the screen:

```
;
;
;                    A program to output characters on the screen.
;
                extrn       exit:far                ;exit to msdos
                extrn       clr:far                 ;procedure to clear screen
code segment
        assume cs:code,ds:t__data,ss:stack
;
;       init segment registers
;
go: mov     ax,t__data
    mov     ds,ax                       ;data segment
    mov     ax,stack
    mov     ss,ax                       ;init ss to stack
    mov     sp,offset s__data           ;set stack pointer
;
;       clear screen
;
    call    clr                         ;clear screen
;
;       display characters
;
    mov     ax,0f000h                   ;load base of screen address
    mov     es,ax                       ;extra segment register = 0f000h
;
;       name__ a is defined in byte mode
;       use 'word ptr' to override the type of the variable
;       defined
;
    mov     ax,word ptr name__a         ;load ascii a
    mov     es:[0],ax                   ;display 'A' on screen
;
    mov     ax,name__c                  ;load 'C' with half intensity
    mov     es:[4],ax                   ;display next ch with 1 space
;
    mov     ah,20h                      ;underline
    mov     al,name__t                  ;load 'T'
    mov     es:[8],ax                   ;display 'T' in underline
;
;       return to msdos
    call    exit
;
codeends
;
;       data segment
;
```

```
t__data     segment
name__a     db  'A'+64h,80h          ;inverse video
name__c     dw  'C'+100+40h*256      ;half intensity
name__t     db  'T'+100              ;underline
t__data     ends
;
stack       segment  stack           ;define stack segment
            db  128   dup(?)          ;size of stack = 128
s__data     equ  $                    ;top of stack
stack       ends                      ;stack segment end
            end  go                   ;end of source file, will
                                      ;begin execution from label go
```

CHAPTER 5

Binary Arithmetic

The 8086/8088 provides the four basic arithmetical operations in a number of different varieties. In both 8-bit and 16-bit operations signed and unsigned arithmetic are provided. Standard two's complement representation of signed values is used.

5.1 ADDITION/SUBTRACTION

ADD – Integer Addition

The result of the add instruction is stored in the destination field, i.e. the first operand, with the status flags altered to reflect the result.

```
add    reg8,reg8           ;reg8 = reg8 + reg8
add    reg8,mem8           ;reg8 = reg8 + mem8
add    reg16,mem16         ;reg16 = reg16 + mem16
add    reg16,reg16         ;reg16 = reg16 + reg16
add    mem8,reg8           ;mem8 = mem8 + reg8
add    mem16,reg16         ;mem16 = mem16 + reg16
```

SUB – Integer Subtraction

SUB subtracts the source operand from the destination operand and returns the difference to the destination field. Status flags are also affected.

```
sub    reg8,reg8           ;reg8 = reg8 – reg8
sub    reg8,mem8           ;reg8 = reg8 – mem8
sub    reg16,reg 16        ;reg16 = reg16 – reg16
sub    reg16,mem16         ;reg16 = reg16 – mem16
sub    mem8,reg8           ;mem8 = mem8 – reg8
sub    mem16,reg16         ;mem16 = mem16 – reg16
```

54

Like the mov instruction, the source operands of the add and sub instructions can be immediate data.

add/sub	reg8,immed8	;reg8 = reg8 +/− immed8
add/sub	mem8,immed8	;mem8 = mem8 +/− immed8
add/sub	reg16,immed16	;reg16 = reg16 +/− immed16
add/sub	mem16,immed16	;mem16 = mem16 +/− immed16

Multiple-Length Arithmetic

For some applications, it is necessary to store numbers greater than 64K which can be represented by 32 bits or more. Each number is stored with the low-order part of the number first, and the high-order part in the next memory locations. That is:

	Low order	High order
address	num,num+1	num+2,num+3

To add two 32-bit numbers together requires the program to execute two add instructions. For example:

```
        num+3,num+2        num+1,num
            0002              ff0e
+           0000              1003
          _____            _____
            0003              0f11
```

To execute in stages, we first add the least significant word together:

```
            ff0e
+           1003
          _____
            0f11          Carry = 1
```

The carry flag is set to reflect the result > 64K.
    The second ADD instruction must include the content of the carry flag:

```
            0002
            0000
+              1          Carry
          _____
               3
```

The 8086/8088 processor provides both adc and sbb which are used for multiple-precision binary arithmetic, where each integer operation includes the content of the carry flag.

```
adc   des,sou                    ;Integer add with carry
sbb   des,sou                    ;Integer subtract with borrow
```

For example:

```
longint1   dw   0ff0eh,   0002h
longint2   dw   01003h,   0000h

mov   ax,longint1               ;longint1 → ax
add   longint2,ax               ;add lower order part
mov   ax,longint1+2             ;longint1+2 → ax
adc   longint2+2,ax            ;add high order part + carry
```

There is also a set of single-operand instructions, such as negate, increment, and decrement. Their mnemonics are:

```
neg   operand             ;negate
inc   operand             ;increment
dec   operand             ;decrement
```

neg subtracts the operand from 0, i.e. taking the two's complement of the operand. Instructions inc and dec are the same as adding or subtracting 1 from the operand. The operand can be reg8, reg16, mem8, or mem16.

```
86add.asm
;
;              examples of binary arithmetic
;
              extrn   exit:far              ;proc to return to msdos
;
code sement                                 ;beginning of segment code
              assume cs:code,ds:t__data,ss:stack
;
;              main module beginning from loc go
;
;              init segment registers
;
go:      mov   ax,t__data          ;address of t__data → ax
         mov   ds,ax               ;init data segment with ax
         mov   ax,stack            ;address of stack → ax
         mov   ss,ax               ;init stack segment with ax
         mov   sp,offset s__data   ;init stack pointer
```

```
;
;              reg/reg
;
               mov    ax,nwd                  ;content of nwd → ax
               mov    bx,nwd2                 ;content of nwd2 → bx
               add    ax,bx                   ;ax = ax + bx
;
;              reg/memory
;
               mov    ax,50                   ;immediate data 50 decimal → ax
               add    ax,conf0                ;ax = ax + content of conf0
;
;              memory/reg
;
               mov    bx,50h                  ;immediate data 50h → bx
               add    nwd,bx                  ;nwd = nwd + bx
;
;              register/immediate
;
               add    bx,10h                  ;bx = bx + 16
;
;              memory-immediate
;
               add    nwd2,10h                ;nwd2 = nwd2 + 16
;
;              return to msdos
               call            exit
;
code           ends
;
;              date segment
;
t__data        segment
nwd            dw              00010H
nwd2           dw              0f0fh
conf0          dw              0f0h
t__data        ends
;
;              stack segment
;
stack          segment         stack
               db              128 dup(?)
s__data        equ             $
stack          ends
               end             go
```

5.2 MULTIPLICATION/DIVISION

With earlier microprocessors, programmers had to write or use algorithms to perform a multiplication and division function. The 8086/8088 processor has both multiply and divide instructions, and uses dedicated registers for their destination register. Only one operand (either a register or a memory location) is required because the first operand is implicitly defined (al, ax or dx:ax).

$$
\begin{array}{rl}
& \text{al} \\
\times \quad & \text{op} \quad \text{(8-bit)} \\
\hline
& \text{ax} \quad \text{(16-bit)}
\end{array}
\qquad
\begin{array}{rl}
& \text{ax} \\
\times \quad & \text{op} \quad \text{(16-bit)} \\
\hline
& \text{dx:ax} \quad \text{(32-bit)}
\end{array}
$$

and

$$
\text{(8-bit)} \quad \text{op} \,\underline{)\ \ \text{ax}}\ -\ \text{remainder} \to \text{ah} \\
\hspace{4.5cm}\text{al}
$$

$$
\text{(16-bit)} \quad \text{op} \,\underline{)\ \ \text{dx:ax}}\ -\ \text{remainder} \to \text{dx} \\
\hspace{4.8cm}\text{ax}
$$

Unsigned Multiplication

```
mul   reg8           ;ax   =   al * reg8
mul   mem8           ;ax   =   al * mem8
mul   reg16          ;dx:ax  =  ax * reg16
mul   mem16          ;dx:ax  =  ax * mem16
```

All operands are 8/16 bit binary numbers.

Signed Multiplication

```
imul   reg8          ;ax  =  al * reg8
imul   mem8          ;ax  =  al * mem8
imul   reg16         ;dx:ax  =  ax * reg16
imul   mem16         ;dx:ax  =  ax * mem16
```

All operands are 7/15 bit binary numbers, the sign of the product having the algebraic value of the two operands, i.e. a negative operand times a negative operand is a positive product. With the destination operand in double length, no overflow can occur.

Unsigned Division

```
div   reg8           ;al   = ax/reg8
```

```
                        ;ah  =  ax mod  reg8
    div    reg16        ;ax  =  dx:ax/reg16
                        ;dx  =  dx:ax mod reg16
    div    mem8
    div    mem16
```

Signed Division

```
    idiv   reg8         ;al  =  ax/reg8 signed division
                        ;ah  =  ax  mod reg8 signed modulo
    idiv   reg16        ;ax  =  dx:ax/ eg16 signed division
                        ;dx  =  dx:ax mod  reg16 signed modulo
    idiv   mem8
    idiv   mem16
```

If the result is too big to fit in the designated register (ax or al) then an interrupt of type 0 is performed to allow the overflow to be handled.

5.3 TYPE CONVERSION

Division works well after a multiplication because the ax or dx:ax registers contain the operands needed to divide by a byte or a word. To extend the dividend to the proper size with its sign extended, the 8086/8088 instruction set has two instructions:

```
    cbw  –  Convert byte in al to word in ax
    cwd  –  Convert word in ax to doubleword in dx:ax
```

These two instructions are used to convert from registers al to ax and ax to dx:ax by sign extension of al and ax. No operand is needed.

```
;
;              example of binary multiplication/division
;
              extrn   gnum:far     ;enter a number from keyboard
              extrn   pnum:far     ;output a binary number in decimal
              extrn   exit:far     ;exit to msdos
code          segment
              assume cs:code,ss:stack
;
;              init segment registers
;
go:           mov     ax,stack
              mov     ss,ax                         ;init ss to stack
              mov     sp,offset  s__data            ;set stack pointer
```

60

```
;
;              convert fahrenheit to celsius
;              result in al with 2 dec
;

               call        gnum              ;read in deg fahr. in ax
;
;              conversion
;

               sub         ax,32             ;f = f−32
               mov         bx,100            ;2 dec places
               imul        bx                ;f = f * 100
;

               mov         cx,5
               imul        cx                ;f = f * 5
;

               mov         cx,9
               idiv        cx                ;f = f/9
;
;              output number in 2 dec
;

               call        pnum              ;output f * 100
;
;              return to msdos
;

               call        exit
;
code           ends
;
stack          segment     stack
               db          128 dup(?)
s__data        equ         $
stack          ends
;

               end         go
```

In this example, there are two more procedures that are defined as externals, namely

    gnum and pnum

Procedure gnum reads a numeric from the keyboard and converts into a binary number in ax. Procedure pnum outputs the content of ax in decimal. All these procedures are defined as far in stdio.asm (see Appendix B).

;

```
;   Example: To accept a pair of xy co-ords as the starting
;   position for the text string output on the screen.
;
            extrn   exit:far                    ;exit to msdos
            extrn   clr:far                     ;clear screen
            extrn   gnum:far                    ;input an integer
            extrn   pstg:far                    ;output a char string
;
;   pstg output a character string terminated by null
;   on entry dx = offset of beginning of character string
;
code        segment
            assume cs:code,ds:t__data,ss:stack
;
;           init segment registers
;
go:         mov     ax,t__data
            mov     ds,ax                       ;data segment
            mov     ax,stack
            mov     ss,ax                       ;init ss to stack
            mov     sp,offset s__data           ;set stack pointer
;
;           clear screen
;
            call    clr                         ;clear screen
;
;           enter x,y co-ord
;
            mov     dx,offset mes1              ;addres of mes1 → dx
            call    pstg                        ;display message
            call    gnum                        ;read × co-ord
            mov     xc,ax                       ;copy × co-ord → xc
            mov     dx,offset mes2              ;address of mes2 → dx
            call    pstg                        ;display message 2
            call    gnum                        ;read y co-ord
            mov     yc,ax                       ;copy y co-ord → yc
;
;           display characters
;
            mov     ax,0f000h                   ;load base of screen address
            mov     es,ax                       ;extra segment register = 0f000h
;
;           calculate start address on screen
;
;           base = y * 160 + × * 2
```

```
;
                mov        ax,yc                        ;row → ax
                mov        cx,160                       ;160 → cx
                imul       cx                           ;y * 160 → dx:ax
                mov        bx,xc                        ;column → bx
                add        bx,bx                        ;2 * column → bx
                add        bx,ax                        ;bx = base offset of string
;
;               output string same as previous example in last chapter
;
                mov        ax,word ptr name__a          ;load ascii a
                mov        es:[bx],ax                   ;display 'A' on screen
                mov        ax,name__c                   ;load 'C'
                mov        es:[bx+4],ax                 ;display 'C'
                mov        ah,20h                       ;underline
                mov        al,name__t                   ;load 'T'
                mov        es:[bx+8],ax                 ;display 'T'
;
;               return to msdos
;
                call       exit                         ;return to op system
code            ends
;
;               data area
;
t__data         segment
name__a  db            'A'+64h,80h                      ;inverse video
name__c  dw            'C'+100+40h*256                  ;half intensity
name__t  db            'T'+100                          ;underline
xc       dw            0
yc       dw            0
mes1     db            'enter x co-ord',0
mes2     db            'enter y co-ord',0
t__data ends
;
;               define stack segments
;
stack           segment    stack
                db         128 dup(?)
s__data         equ        $
stack           ends
                end        go
```

CHAPTER 6

Logical Instructions

6.1 LOGICAL INSTRUCTIONS

The 8086/8088 can perform four of the logical operations NOT, AND, OR, and exclusive OR. Like the arithmetic instructions, each type of logical operation can have 10 types of operands, i.e. reg, immediate data, and memory address in 8-bit and 16-bit modes. That is:

and	reg8,reg8	;reg8 = reg8 & reg8
and	reg8,mem8	;reg8 = reg8 & mem8
and	reg16,reg16	;reg16 = reg16 & reg16
and	reg16,mem16	;reg16 = reg16 & mem16
and	mem8,reg8	;mem8 = mem8 & reg8
and	mem16,reg16	;mem16 = mem16 & reg16
and	reg8,immed8	;reg8 = reg8 & immed8
and	mem8,immed8	;mem8 = mem8 & immed8
and	reg16,immed16	;reg16 = reg16 & immed16
and	mem16,immed16	;mem16 = mem16 & immed16

The result of each instruction is stored in the destination field with the status flags changed according to the result. There is a similar set of instructions for the other logical operations:

	or	s	;logical or
and			
	xor	s	;logical exclusive or

AND

The AND operation is characterized by the fact that the output is '1' only if both inputs are '1'. One of the important uses of the AND instruction is to clear (maskoff) one or more specified bit positions in a byte. The carry flag and

63

overflow flag are cleared. For example, to clear the top 4 bits in memory loc data:

      and   data,00001111b   ;mask mem with immediate data 0f

before execution,

```
    data  =  10101010
    mask  =  00001111
                ─────────
after           00001010
```

i.e. the left-hand 4 bits are cleared, the right-hand 4 bits are preserved.

OR

The OR operation results in a '1' if one of the inputs is '1'. This therefore is used most frequently to set any bit in a byte to '1'. The carry flag and overflow flag are set. For example, to set the lower 4 bits in memory location data:

      or   data,00001111b   ;set bits

before execution,

```
    data  =  10101010
    mask  =  00001111
                ─────────
after           10101111
```

i.e. the left-hand 4 bits are preserved, the right-hand 4 bits are set.

XOR

The XOR operation is used for comparison of two bits of data. If either bit is different, the exclusive OR of the data will be nonzero. To operate an XOR with itself clears the data whereas XOR with 0ffh complements the data. Both the carry flag and overflow flag are cleared. For example, complement data:

      xor   data,11111111b

before execution,

```
    data  =  01010101
    mask  =  11111111
                ─────────
after           10101010
```

i.e. the data is complemented.

The ability to manipulate bits in a byte means that information can be compacted together.

NOT

The 8086/8088 processor provides another instruction in complementing an operand, i.e. the operand is inverted, so that every 1 becomes a 0 and vice versa.

not	reg8	;reg = 1's complement of reg8
not	mem8	;reg = 1's complement of mem8
not	reg16	;reg = 1's complement of reg16
not	mem16	;reg = 1's complement of mem16

6.2 SHIFT AND ROTATE INSTRUCTIONS

The shift and rotate instructions work on bytes or words. Each instruction has two forms: single-bit and variable-bit. The single-bit shift and rotate instructions execute on a single bit as the 8-bit processor. The variable-bit shift and rotate instructions utilize the cl register in order to hold the variable shift or rotate count. Because the processor takes a copy of the content of the cl register, and decrements it internally, cl contains the same data after the operation as it did before.

Shift

The shift instruction will move the content of the operand by one bit or by count in cl to the left or to the right:

sal	reg8,1	;shift reg8 by 1
sal	mem8,1	;shift mem8 by 1
sal	reg16,1	;shift reg16 by 1
sal	mem16,1	;shift mem16 by 1
sal	reg8,cl	;shift reg8 by count in cl
sal	mem8,cl	;shift mem8 by count in cl
sal	reg16,cl	;shift reg16 by count in cl
sal	mem16,cl	;shift mem16 by count in cl

The specified destination operand is shift left. Its most significant bit replaces the carry flag. All other bits in the destination are shifted. The least significant bit is filled with 0. Instructions SHL (shift left logical) and SAL (shift left arithmetic) have the same binary opcode and therefore produce identical results.

There are also two shift right instructions:

```
sar   s                      ;arithmetic shift right
shr   s                      ;logical shift right
```

With the arithmetic shift right instruction, the specified destination operand is shift right. Its least significant bit replaces the carry flag. All other bits in the destination are shifted. The most significant bit retains its old value. With the logical shift right instruction, the most significant bit is always filled with 0. For example:

```
    sal   bl,1               ;logical shift left 1 bit
before,
    bl = 10101010            carry flag = 0
after
    bl = 01010100            carry flag = 1


    sar   bx,1               ;logical shift right 1 bit
before,
    bl = 10101010            carry flag = 1
after,
    bl = 01010101            carry flag = 0


    shr   bx,1               ;arith shift right 1 bit
before,
    bl = 10101010            carry flag = 0
after,
    bl = 11010101            carry flag = 0
```

Rotate

Two types of rotate instructions are provided, i.e. rotate, and rotate through carry. Each instruction can be of two different forms as in the shift instructions:

```
    rol   reg8,1             ;rotate reg8 left by 1
    rol   mem8,1             ;rotate mem8 left by 1
    rol   reg16,1            ;rotate reg16 left by 1
    rol   mem16,1            ;rotate mem16 left by 1

    rol   reg8,cl            ;rotate reg8 left by count in c
    rol   mem8,cl            ;rotate mem8 left by count in cl
    rol   reg16,cl           ;rotate reg16 left by count in cl
    rol   mem16,cl           ;rotate mem16 left by count in cl
and
```

```
ror   s                              ;rotate right
rcl   s                              ;rotate left through carry
rcr   s                              ;rotate right through carry
```

Each operation is as shown in Figure 6.1.

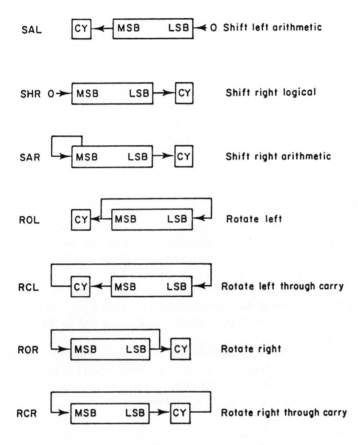

6.1 8086 shift and rotate instructions.

For example:

```
          rcr   dl,1               ;rotate right
before    dl = 01010101           carry = 0
after     di = 00101010           carry = 1

          rcl   dl,1               ;rotate left through carry
before    dl = 10101010           carry = 0
after     dl = 01010100           carry = 0
```

Although the 8086 processor has multiply and divide instructions, they are relatively slow compared with the shift instructions. For example, to multiply a binary integer in reg ax

(i) using arithmetic instruction MUL

mov cx,5	;5 → cx	4
mul cx	;cx * ax → dx:ax	118
	;total clock cycle	122

(ii) using shift and add instructions,

mov dx,ax	;make a copy of ax	4
sal ax,1	;ax = ax * 2	2
sal ax,1	;ax = ax * 4	2
add ax,dx	;ax = ax * 5	+ 3
	;total clock cycle	11

Bit-maps

A bit-map is a string of 1s and 0s. Each member of the bit-map has a position and a value 0 or 1. Bit-maps are data structures that can speed data-handling and reduce memory requirements in a variety of programming applications.

In modern graphic display, a bit-mapping technique is used to store a rectangular array of picture elements, or pixels. In the simplest case, one can represent black and white images with 1s and 0s. Thus a 16×16 array of black and white pixels could be represented by values stored in the 16×16-bit memory map.

The bit-mapping technique is also used in the representation of disk sector usage. Disk sectors, or multiple sectors, are numbered in sequence 0,1,...,n. Each unit is a single bit in the bit-map. While the disk unit is in use, the corresponding bit is set. The operating system uses this bit-map to find the next empty sector for disk write.

To set a bit in memory, load cl with the bit number (least significant bit, lsb = 0, and most significant bit, msb = 15):

mov	dx,1	;set mask = 1
shl	dx,cl	;shift mask to required bit
or	mem,dx	;set bit in mem

Similarly, to clear a bit in memory:

mov	dx,1	;set mask to 1
shl	dx,cl	;shift mask to required bit
not	dx	;set mask to 0
and	mem,dx	;clear bit

For a 256 × 256 high-resolution graphic terminal, the size of the bit-map = 256 * 256/16 words. If the x,y coordinates are defined with (0,0) as the top left-hand corner, each line is 16 (256/16) words and each word is 16 pixels. That is, pixel (x,y) is specified by y*256/16 + x/16 from the beginning of the bit-map buffer.

$$(x,y)=(0,0)$$

The instructions needed to set a pixel specified by x,y are:

```
        mov   bx,offset mem        ;first element of bit-maps
        mov   ax,ycord             ;y co-ord → ax
        mov   cl,4                 ;4 → cl
        shl   ax,cl                ;y * 16 = offset from beginning
        add   bx,ax                ;address of line
        mov   ax,xcord             ;x co-ord → ax
        mov   cl,4                 ;4 → cl
        shr   ax,cl                ;x div 16 = offset from line
        add   bx,ax                ;address of word
        mov   cx,xcord             ;x co-ord → cx
        and   cx,15                ;cl mod 16
        mov   dx,8000h             ;set mask = 8000h
        shr   dx,cl                ;shift mask to required bit
        or    [bx],dx              ;set bit in mem
;
;   Example: To accept a pair of xy co-ords as the starting
;   position for the text string output on the screen.
;
        extrn    exit:far          ;exit to msdos
        extrn    clr:far           ;clear screen
        extrn    gnum:far          ;input an integer
        extrn    pstg:far          ;output a char string
;
code    segment
        assume cs:code,ds:t__data,ss:stack
;
;       init segment registers
;
go:     mov      ax,t__data
        mov      ds,ax             ;data segment
        mov      ax,stack
        mov      ss,ax             ;init ss to stack
```

```
        mov      sp,offset s__data      ;set stack pointer
;
;       clear screen
;
        call     clr                    ;clear screen
;
;       enter x,y co-ord
;
        mov      dx,offset mes1         ;address of mes1 → dx
        call     pstg                   ;display message
        call     gnum                   ;read × co-ord
        mov      xc,ax                  ;copy × co-ord → xc
        mov      dx,offset mes2         ;address of mes2 → dx
        call     pstg                   ;display message 2
        call     gnum                   ;read y co-ord
        mov      yc,ax                  ;copy y co-ord → yc
;
;       display characters
;
        mov      ax,0f000h              ;load base of screen address
        mov      es,ax                  ;extra segment register = 0f000h
;
;       calculate start address on screen
;       this program replaces the imul instruction
;       with a number of shift instructions
;       total number of cycles are approx. 1/3 of using imul
;
;       base = y * 160 + x * 2
;            = y * 32 * 5 + x * 2
;
;
        mov      ax,yc                  ;row → ax
        mov      cl,5                   ;5 → cl
        shl      ax,cl                  ;ax * 32 → ax
        mov      bx,ax                  ;ax → bx
        shl      ax,1                   ;ax * 2 → ax
        shl      ax,1                   ;ax * 2 → ax
        add      ax,bx                  ;row * 160 → ax
        mov      bx,xc                  ;column → bx
        shl      bx,1                   ;2 * column → bx
        add      bx,ax                  ;bx = base offset of string
;
;       output string same as previous example in last chapter
;
        mov      ax,word ptr name__a    ;load ascii a
        mov      es:[bx],ax             ;display 'A' on screen
```

```
        mov       ax,name__c                      ;load 'C'
        mov       es:[bx+4],ax                    ;display 'C'
        mov       ah,20h                          ;underline
        mov       al,name__t                      ;load 'T'
        mov       es:[bx+8],ax                    ;display 'T'
;
;       return to msdos
;
        call      exit                            ;return to op system
code    ends
;
;       data area
;
t__data segment
name__a db        'A'+64h,80h                     ;inverse video
name__c dw        'C'+100+40h*256                 -half intensity
name__t db        'T'+100                         ;underline
xc      dw        0
yc      dw        0
mes1    db        'enter x co-ord',0
mes2    db        'enter y co-ord',0
t__data ends
;
;       define stack segment
;
stack   segment   stack
        db        128 dup(?)
s__data equ       $
stack   ends
        end       go
```

CHAPTER 7

Branching

Instructions are fetched from the memory using the cs register and the ip register. The program-transfer instructions can change the contents of both the cs and ip registers (use when transfer to a new code segment) or just the ip register.

7.1 UNCONDITIONAL BRANCHING

Intra-segment

jmp	label	;branch within segment, ;label is defined within the segment ;as near ;this instruction is 3-byte long
jmp	reg16	;branch within segment indirectly, ;offset specified by the content ;of the reg16
jmp	short label	;branch within 127 bytes, ;only 2-byte in length
jmp	word ptr [pointer]	;indirect branch within segment, ;offset specified by the content ;of (pointer)
jmp	label[pointer]	;branch indirectly, ;offset specified by the content of ;table[pointer]

Inter-segment

jmp	label	;branch to label in another segment ;label has been defined as far ;this instruction is 5 byte long

```
        jmp   far     ptr  label            ;branch to label in another segment
                                            ;label has been defined as near in
                                            ;another segment
        jmp   dword   ptr  [pointer]        ;indirect branch to another
                                            ;segment, offset specified by
                                            ;the content of (pointer)
```

Example 1

```
;
;           unconditional branch within segment
;
1__0:       mov  ax,0
            jmp  1__2                       ;1__2 declared as near
;
1__2:       mov  ax,2
            jmp  short 1__4                 ;1__4 is within 127 byte
;
;           indirectly
;
1__4:       mov  bx,offset 1__6            ;load address → bx
            jmp  bx                         ;jump to address specified by
                                            ;bx
;
1__6:       mov  ax,30
            mov  bx,offset  1__ptr         ;load ptr address
            jmp  word     ptr  [bx]        ;branch indirectly to address
                                            ;specified by content of bx
;
1__30:      jmp  1__0
;
;           inter-segment unconditionally
;
            jmp  fl__2                      ;fl__2 declared as far
;
;           indirectly
;
            mov  bx,offset fl__ptr         ;load ptr address
            jmp  dword ptr [bx]             ;branch indirectly
                                            ;double word address
                                            ;i.e. both offset and segment
                                            ;base value
;
;           data segment
;
```

```
1__ptr     dw    1__30                  ;offset of 1__30 from code
fl__ptr    dd    far__label             ;offset of far__label from
                                        ;another segment base addr.
                                        ;+ segment base value
```

Note especially the difference between

```
jmp    bx                              ;branch from register bx
jmp    word    ptr [bx]                ;branch from a word variable which is
                                       ;pointed at by the register
```

and

```
jmp    dword   ptr [bx]                ;branch from a double word variable
                                       ;which is pointed at by the register
```

(See Figure 7.1.)

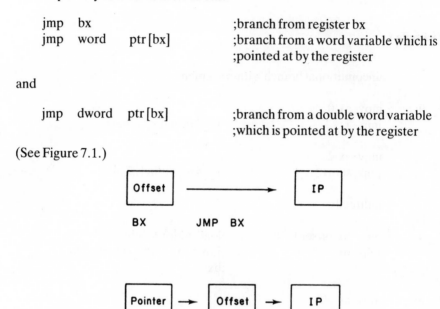

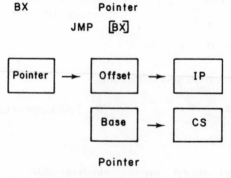

7.1 Indirect branching.

Example 2

Indirect branching can be used where there is menu driven software. An example of a communication package could have screen as follows:

[0]   exit
[1]   transmit
[2]   receive
[3]   directory on this terminal
[4]   directory on remote terminal

Enter selection:

The program branches to different routines according to the keyboard entry. Such programs are often written with a jump table and the indirect branch instruction.

To use the indirect addressing mode

```
jmp   bx
```

each entrance in the jump table is three bytes long, i.e.

```
jtable:   jmp   l__exit
          jmp   l__trans
          jmp   l__rec
          jmp   l__dir__this
          jmp   l__dir__other
```

and the main program control is

```
call   gnum                ;read option in ax
mov    bx,ax               ;made a copy
shl    ax,1                ;ax * 2
add    ax,bx               ;ax = ax * 3
mov    bx,offset jtable    ;beginning of jump table
add    bx,ax               ;point to new address
jmp    bx                  ;jump to option
```

Using jmp [bx], the jump table could be reduced to 2 bytes per entry:

```
;
;          unconditional branch using table
;          depending on the value of ax,
;
;          the next instruction executed after
;          jmp jtable[bx]
;          will be l__exit, l__trans, l__rec, l–dir__this, or
;                  l__dir__other
;
1__00:     call   gnum                ;read number in ax
           shl    ax,1                ;ax = ax * 2
           mov    bx,ax               ;mov to pointer
```

```
        jmp jtable[bx]                    ;jump with number
;
l__exit     label       near
        .................
l__trans    label       near
        .................
l__rec      label       near
        .................
l__dir__this            label       near
        .................
l__dir__other           label       near
        .................
;
;           data definitions
;
jtable      dw    l__exit
            dw    l__trans
            dw    l__rec
            dw    l__dir__this
            dw    l__dir__other
```

7.2 COMPARE INSTRUCTIONS

There are two compare instructions in 8086/8088:

```
        cmp   op1,op2                  ;compare two operands
```

and

```
        test  op1,op2                  ;logical compare
```

Compare Two Operands

The flags are set by the subtraction of the right operand from the left operand. Neither operand is modified:

```
        cmp   reg8,reg8           ;flags = reg8 − reg8
        cmp   reg8,mem8           ;flags = reg8 − mem8
        cmp   reg16,reg16         ;flags = reg16 − reg16
        cmp   reg16,mem16         ;flags = reg16 − mem16
        cmp   mem8,reg8           ;flags = mem8 − reg8
        cmp   mem16,reg16         ;flags = mem16 − reg16

        cmp   reg8,immed8         ;flags = reg8 − immed8
        cmp   mem8,immed8         ;flags = mem8 − immed8
        cmp   reg16,immed16       ;flags = reg16 − immed16
        cmp   mem16,immed16       ;flags = mem16 − immed16
```

```
cmp    reg16,immed8          ;flags = reg16 − immed8
cmp    mem16,immed8          ;flags = mem16 − immed8
```

Logical Compare

The flags are set as the result of a bitwise logical and of the two operands. Neither operand is modified:

```
test    reg8,reg8             ;flags = reg8 and reg8
test    reg8,mem8             ;flags = reg8 and mem8
test    reg16,reg16           ;flags = reg16 and reg16
test    reg16,mem16           ;flags = reg16 and mem8

test    mem8,immed8           ;flags = mem8 and immed8
test    reg8,immed8           ;flags = reg8 and immed8
test    mem16,immed16         ;flags = mem16 and immed16
test    reg16,immed16         ;flags = reg16 and immed16
```

Apart from the two compare instructions, Table 7.1 shows other instructions that modify the conditional flags.

7.3 CONDITIONAL BRANCHING

Conditional jump instructions are used to test the status flags, which have been set by a previous instruction. The 8086/8088 assembler allows different mnemonics for each interpretation to aid documentation purposes.

In every case, if the condition specified in the conditional jump is true, the signed displacement byte is sign extended to a word and added to the ip, which has been updated to point to the first byte of the next instruction. This limits the range of the conditional jump to 127 (decimal) bytes beyond and 126 bytes before the instruction. Conditional jumps to instructions outside the range can be made by a conditional jump followed by an unconditional jump:

```
ja      label    ;jump if above (cf or zf) = 0
jae     label    ;jump if above or equal (cf = 0)
jb      label    ;jump if below (cf = 1)
jbe     label    ;jump if below or equal (cf or zf) = 1
jc      label    ;jump if carry set (cf = 1)
je      label    ;jump if equal (zf = 1)
jg      label    ;jump if greater ((sf xor of) or zf) = 0
jge     label    ;jump if greater or equal (sf xor of) = 0
jl      label    ;jump if less (sf xor of) = 1
jle     label    ;jump if less or equal ((sf xor of) or zf) = 1
jna     label    ;jump if not above (cf or zf) = 1
jnae    label    ;jump if neither above nor equal (cf = 1)
jnb     label    ;jump if not below (cf = 0)
jnbe    label    ;jump if neither below nor equal (cf or zf) = 0
jnc     label    ;jump if no carry (cf = 0)
jne     label    ;jump if not equal (zf = 0)
```

78

Table 7.1

Instruction	Flags						
	O	S	Z	A	P	C	
ADC	X	X	X	X	X	X	O – Overflow flag
ADD	X	X	X	X	X	X	S – Sign
AND	0	X	X	U	X	0	Z – Zero
CBW	—	—	—	—	—	—	A – Auxiliary carry
CLC	—	—	—	—	—	0	P – Parity
CMC	—	—	—	—	—	X	C – Carry
CMP	X	X	X	X	X	X	
CWD	—	—	—	—	—	—	
DIV	U	U	U	U	U	U	
IDIV	U	U	U	U	U	U	
IMUL	X	U	U	U	U	X	
INC	X	X	X	X	X	—	
Jcond	—	—	—	—	—	—	
JMP	—	—	—	—	—	—	
LDS	—	—	—	—	—	—	
LEA	—	—	—	—	—	—	
LES	—	—	—	—	—	—	
LOOP	—	—	—	—	—	—	
MOV	—	—	—	—	—	—	
MUL	X	U	U	U	U	X	
NEG	X	X	X	X	X	X	
NOP	—	—	—	—	—	—	
NOT	—	—	—	—	—	—	
OR	0	X	X	U	X	0	
RCL	X	—	—	—	—	X	
RCR	X	—	—	—	—	X	
ROL	X	—	—	—	—	X	
ROR	X	—	—	—	—	X	
SAL/SHL	X	—	—	—	—	X	
SAR	X	X	X	U	X	X	
SBB	X	X	X	X	X	X	
SHR	X	—	—	—	—	X	
STC	—	—	—	—	—	1	
SUB	X	X	X	X	X	X	
TEST	0	X	X	U	X	0	
XCHG	—	—	—	—	—	—	
XOR	0	X	X	U	X	0	

X Modified by the instruction; result depends on operands.
– Not modified.
U Undefined after the instruction.
1 Set to 1 by the instruction.
0 Clear to 0 by the instruction.

jng	label	;jump if not greater ((sf xor of) or zf) = 1
jnge	label	;jump if not greater nor equal (sf xor of) = 1
jnl	label	;jump if not less (sf xor of) = 0
jnle	label	;jump if not less nor equal (JG)
jno	label	;jump if no overflow (of = 0)
jnp	label	;jump if no parity (pf = 0)
jns	label	;jump if positive (sf = 0)
jnz	label	;jump if not zero (zf = 0)
jo	label	;jump if overflow (of = 1)
jp	label	;jump if parity (pf = 1)
jpe	label	;jump if parity even (pf = 1)
jpo	label	;jump if parity odd (pf = 0)
js	label	;jump if sign (sf = 1)
jz	label	;jump if zero (zf = 1)
jcxz	label	;jump if cx is zero

These instructions can be divided into three main groups, as shown in Table 7.2.

Table 7.2

Mnemonic	Jump if
jg/jnle	greater/not lesser equal
jge/jnl	greater or equal/not less
jl/jnge	less/not greater nor equal
jle/jng	less or equal/not greater
jo	overflow
js	sign
jno	not overflow
jns	not sign
Unsigned	
ja/jnbe	above/not below nor equal
jae/jnb	above or equal/not below
jb/jnae	below/not above nor equal
jbe/jna	below or equal/not above
Either	
jc	carry
je/jz	equal/zero
jp/jpe	parity/parity even
jnc	not carry
jne/jnz	not equal/not zero
jnp/jpo	not parity/parity odd

Carry Flag Operations

The carry flag can be altered via three different operations:

```
clc          ;clears the cf flag
cmc          ;complements the cf flag
stc          ;sets the cf flag
```

Example 1

To check if al contains a '−' sign; if yes, change the content of dx to −dx:

```
cmp   al,'−'           ;if al eq '−'
jne   no__change
neg   dx               ;dx = −dx

no__change label     near

   mov   number, dx      ;store dx
```

Example 2

To find the larger number and store the larger one in loc max:

```
         mov     ax,data1       ;load data1 in ax
         cmp     ax,data2       ;compare with data2
         jg      no__change     ;if data1 > data2
         mov     ax,data2

no__change   label   near
             mov     max,ax
```

Example 3

A case statement in lang C.

```
switch (type) {
      case 'U':     row−−;         /*if type = 'U', dec row */
                    break;
      case 'D':     row++;         /* if type = 'D', inc row */
                    break;
      case 'L':     col−−          /* if type = 'L', dec col */
                    break;
      case 'R':     col++;         /* if type = 'R' inc col */
}                                  /* no default case */
```

is equivalent to a group of IF statements in BASIC:

```
IF TYPE = 'U' GOTO   100
IF TYPE = 'D' GOTO   200
```

The same routine in assembly language could be written as:

```
                mov     al,type         ;load type in al
                cmp     al,'U'          ;if type = 'U'
                jne     l__case1
                dec     row             ;row = row − 1
                jmp     l__endcase
;
l__case1:       cmp     al,'D'          ;if type = 'D'
                jne     l__case2
                inc     row             ;row = row + 1
                jmp     l__endcase
;
l case2:        cmp     al,'L'          ;if type = 'L'
                jne     l__case3
                dec     col             ;col = col − 1
                jmp     l__endcase
;
l__case3:       cmp     al,'R'          ;if type = 'R'
                jne     l__endcase
                inc     col             ;col = col + 1
;
l__endcase      label   near
```

Example 4

To replace a conditional jump to another segment:

```
                jz      far__label      ;must be replaced by
                jnz     l__skip
l__skip         label   near

                jmp     far__label
                ..............
```

```
;
;
;               Write a program to validate a date entry and output
;               the following date.
;
;
;
```

```
        extrn   exit:far                ;exit to msdos
        extrn   gnum:far                ;input an integer
        extrn   pnum:far                ;output an integer
        extrn   putc:far                ;output a char
        extrn   pstg:far                ;output a char string
        extrn   pline:far               ;output a cr,lf
;
code    segment
        assume  cs:code,ds:t__data,ss:stack
;
;       init    segment  registers
;
go:     mov     ax,t__data
        mov     ds,ax                   ;data segment
        mov     ax,stack
        mov     ss,ax                   ;init ss to stack
        mov     sp,offset s__data       ;set stack pointer
;
;       read date
;
retry:  mov     dx,offset mes1          ;address of mes1 → dx
        call    pstg                    ;display message
        call    gnum                    ;read in date
        mov     date,ax                 ;ax → date
;
        mov     dx,offset mes2          ;address of mes2 → dx
        call    pstg                    ;display message
        call    gnum                    ;read in month
        mov     month,ax                ;ax → month
;
        mov     dx,offset mes3          ;address of mes3 → dx
        call    pstg                    ;display message
        call    gnum                    ;read in year
        mov     year,ax                 ;ax → year
;
;       validate month and date
;
        mov     bx,31                   ;31 days in month
        mov     ax,month                ;check month
        cmp     ax,2                    ;compare with 2
        jz      feb                     ;treat feb specially
;
        cmp     ax,4                    ;compare with 4
        jz      sh__month               ;short month
```

```
        cmp        ax,6                    ;6?
        jz         sh__month               ;yes, short month
        cmp        ax,9                    ;is it 9
        jz         sh__month               ;yes, short month
        cmp        ax,11                   ;is it 11
        jz         sh__month               ;yes, short month
        jmp        valid__date             ;max day in month = 31
;                                          ;branch to validation
;          short month
;
sh__month label     near
        mov        bx,30                   ;only 30 day in month
        jmp        valid__date             ;branch to validation
;
;          feb
;
feb        label    near
        mov        bx,28                   ;default to 28
        mov        ax,year                 ;year → ax
        test       ax,3                    ;year mod 4, is it 0
        jnz        valid__date             ;no, branch to validation
        mov        bx,29                   ;leap year
;
;          validate date of month
;          assume all numbers are positive and non zero
;          could also include validation of year and month
;
valid__date         label    near
        mov        ax,date                 ;date → ax
        cmp        ax,bx                   ;compare with max day of month
        jle        next__date              ;valid day, branch to nextdate
;
;          output error message
;
        mov        dx,offset mes4          ;address of mes4 → dx
        call       pstg                    ;display message
        jmp        retry                   ;unconditional branch to retry
;
;          evaluate next day
;
next__date          label    near
        inc        date                    ;date + 1 → date
        cmp        date,bx                 ;is it end of month
        jle        l__out                  ;no, jump to l__out
```

```
;
;              next month/day = 1
;
              mov      date,1              ;1st of month → date
              inc      month              ;next month
              cmp      month,12           ;is it end of year
              jle      l__out             ;no, jump to l__out
;
;              next year / month = 1
;
              mov      month,1            ;Jan → month
              inc      year               ;next year
;
;              output string in dd/mm/yy
;
l__out:       call     pline              ;output cr,lf
              mov      dx,offset mes5     ;address of mes5 → dx
              call     pstg               ;display message
              mov      ax,date            ;date → ax
              call     pnum               ;display date
              mov      al,'/'             ;'/' → al
              call     putc               ;display '/'
              mov      ax,month           ;month → ax
              call     pnum               ;display month
              mov      al,'/'             ;'/' → al
              call     putc               ;display '/'
              mov      ax,year            ;year → ax
              call     pnum               ;display year
;
;              return to msdos
;
              call     exit
code          ends
;
;              data area
;
t__data       segment
mes1          db       'enter date ',0
mes2          db       'enter month ',0
mes3          db       'enter year ',0
mes4          db       'invalid date, please retry ',0ah, 0dh, 0
mes5          db       'next day is ',0
date          dw       0
month         dw       0
year          dw       0
```

```
t__data    ends
;
stack      segment    stack
           db         128 dup(?)
s__data    equ        $
stack      ends
;
           end        go
```

CHAPTER 8

Looping

8.1 LOOPING

The LOOP instruction is intended to provide iteration control and combine loop index management with conditional branching. To use the loop instruction it is necessary to load an unsigned iteration count into cx, then code the loop at the end of the series of instructions to be iterated. Each time loop is executed the cx register is decremented and a conditional branch to the top of the loop is performed.

```
loop    label              ;decrement the cx register by one
                           ;and branches if cx is not zero
```

Except that no flags are affected by the loop instruction, it is equivalent to

```
dec  cx                    ;decrement cx
jnz  label                 ;branches if zero flag is not set
```

The mnemonic 'loop' is often used as a label in most assembly language programs, but must definitely be avoided in 8086.

Because the loop instruction does not affect the zero flag, one can precede the instruction with a compare instruction and make it a conditional loop. There are two conditional loop instructions:

```
loopz    label             ;decrement the cx register by one
                           ;and branches if cx is not zero
                           ;and the zf flag is set
loope    label             ;same as loopz
loopnz   label             ;decrement the cx register by one
                           ;and branches if cx is not zero
                           ;and the zf flag is cleared.
loopne   label             ;same as loopnz
```

86

In every case, if the condition specified in the conditional loop is true, the instruction with 'label' is executed. The instruction format of these instructions limits the range of the conditional loop to 127 bytes beyond and 126 bytes before the instruction.

Examples

1. A delay loop:

```
            mov   cx,0ffffh        ;loop count = 0ffffh → cx
d__loop:    nop                    ;3 clock cycle per loop
            loop d__loop           ;loop till cx = 0
```

2. To output a line of 10 ×'s on the screen:

```
        mov   cx,10            ;length of display → cx = 10
        mov   ax,0f000h        ;screen buffer address → ax
        mov   es,ax            ;set es
        mov   ax,'X'+100       ;set char
        mov   bx,0             ;set base address to 0
;
lp:     mov   es:[bx],ax       ;place char in display area
        inc   bx               ;increment bx twice
        inc   bx               ;     i.e. in word mode
        loop  lp               ;dec cx and repeat until cx = 0
```

3. Use of jcxz.

If register cx is not checked for zero before the loop, there is a risk of executing the loop 64K times. To prevent this, the JCXZ (jump on cx is zero) instruction can be used. It branches to the label specified if cx is equal to zero and will not execute the loop at all.

```
            jcxz   l__end              ;no exec of loop if cx is 0
l__00:      mov    byte ptr [bx],al    ;store byte
            inc    bx                  ;next byte
            loop   l__00
l__end      label  near
```

```
;
;
;           Write a program to output a table of c/f
;           conversion. C ranges from −10 to 20.
;
;

            extrn   pstg:far
            extrn   pnum:far
            extrn   putc:far
            extrn   pline:far
```

88

```
                extrn    exit:far
code            segment
                assume cs:code,ds:t__data,ss:stack
go:             mov      ax,t__data
                mov      ds,ax                      ;init ds to t__data
                mov      ax,stack
                mov      ss,ax                      ;init ss to stack
                mov      sp,offset s__data          ;set stack pointer
;
;               convert celsius to fahrenheit
;               result in al with 2 dec
;
                mov      dx,offset mes              ;address of mes → dx
                call     pstg                       ;display message
                mov      cx,30                      ;−10 to 10
mlop:           mov      ax,cent                    ;cent → ax
                call     pnum                       ;display cent
                mov      al,' '                     ;sp → al
                call     putc                       ;display space
                mov      al,'='                     ;-'=' → al
                call     putc                       ;display '='
                mov      al,' '                     ;sp → al
                call     putc                       ;display space
;
;               conversion
;
                mov      ax,cent                    ;cent → ax
                mov      dx,180                     ;180 → dx
                imul     dx                         ;c * 1.80 → dx:ax
;
                add      ax,3200                    ;c * 1.80 + 32.00 → ax
                cwd                                 ;convert to doubleword
                mov      bx,100                     ;calculate dec., fractions
                idiv     bx                         ;integer part in ax
                                                    ;fractions in dx
                call     pnum                       ;output integer part
                mov      al,'.'                     ;load '.'
                call     putc                       ;output '.'
                cmp      dx,10                      ;check need extra zero
                jge      lnext                      ;skip output '0'
                mov      al,'0'                     ;load '0'
                call     putc                       ;output '0'
lnext:          mov      ax,dx                      ;dx → ax
                call     pnum                       ;output fraction
                call     pline                      ;output newline
```

```
;
            inc       cent                          ;next degree
            loop      mlop                          ;repeated until cx = 0
;
;           return to msdos
;
            call      exit
code        ends
;
;           data
;
t__data     segment
cent        dw        −10
mes         db        'cent    feri',0ah,0dh,0
t__data     ends
;
stack       segment   stack
            db        128 dup(?)
s__data     equ       $
stack       ends
;
            end       go


;
;           Output a monthly calendar for Jan given the 1st day of month
;
;

            extrn     pstg:far
            extrn     pnum:far
            extrn     putc:far
            extrn     pline:far
            extrn     gnum:far
            extrn     exit:far

LF          equ       0ah
CR          equ       0dh
;
code        segment
            assume cs:code,ds:t__data,ss:stack
go:         mov       ax,t__data
            mov       ds,ax                         ;init ds to t__data
            mov       ax,stack
            mov       ss,ax                         ;init ss to stack
            mov       sp,offset s__data             ;set stack pointer
;
```

```
;               enter first day of month
;
                mov     dx,offset mes            ;load offset of mes
                call    pstg                     ;output question
                call    gnum                     ;sun to sat (0–6)
;
;               output heading
;
                mov     dx,offset heading        ;load offset of heading
                call    pstg                     ;output JAN
;
;               output leading spaces
;
                mov     day,ax                   ;ax → day
                inc     day                      ;start from 1
;
                mov     cx,ax                    ;copy to count
                jcxz    l_date
;
                mov     al,' '                   ;load space in al
l_sp:           call    putc                     ;output space
                call    putc                     ;output space
                call    putc                     ;output space
                loop    l_sp                     ;repeat for sun,mon…
;
;               output date in mod 7
;
l_date:         mov     cx,31                    ;max day of month
                mov     word  ptr  date,1        ;date start from 1st of Jan
;
l_main:         cmp     word  ptr  date,10       ;less than 10, need extra sp
                jge     l_next
                mov     al,' '                   ;load space in al
                call    putc
;
l_next:         mov     ax,date
                call    pnum
;
                inc     date
                inc     day
                and     word  ptr  day,7
                jnz     l_new
;
;               output new line when Sun.
;
                call    pline
```

```
              inc    day                        ;start from 1 again
l__new:       loop   l__main
;
;             return to msdos
;
              call   exit
code          ends
;
;             data
;
t__data       segment
mes           db     'Enter first day of month (0–6 for Sun to Sat)',0
heading       db     '    JAN',CR,LF
              db     ' S M T W T F S',CR,LF,0
date          dw     0
day           dw     0
t__data       ends
;
stack         segmentstack
              db     128 dup(?)
s__data       equ    $
stack         ends
              end    go
```

8.2 ARRAYS

In the above example, the register bx is used to index through an array of memory locations. The 8086/8088 provides three indirect memory addressing modes:

1.   Base addressing   [bx+displacement]
                                       [bp+displacement]
       i.e.   content of base register + constant
2.   Indexed addressing   variable [si]
                                        variable [di]
       i.e.   offset + content of index reg.
3.   Based indexed addressing   [bx+si]
                                          [bx][di][2]
       i.e.   content of base reg.
                                  + content of index reg.
                                  + constant displacement

Note that [bx+bp] or [si+di] are not valid.

1. To add two arrays of integers:

```
              mov      cx,10          ;no of elements → cx = 10
              mov      si,0           ;initialize source index
              mov      di,0           ;initialize des index
    ;
    l__lp:    mov      ax,datab[si]   ;load datab → ax
              add      dataa[di],ax   ;da[i] = da[i] + db[i]
              inc      si             ;increment source index in
              inc      si             ;   word mode
              inc      di             ;increment destination index in
              inc      di             ;   word mode
              loop     l__lp          ;loop till count in cx = 0
    ;
    dataa     dw       10 dup(?)      ;reserve 10 words for dataa
    datab     dw       10 dup(?)      ;reserve 10 words for datab
```

2. To pack one array in word mode to byte mode:

```
              mov      cx,10          ;no of elements to be pack → cx
              mov      si,0           ;initialize source index
              mov      di,0           ;initialize des index
    ;
    l__lp:    mov      ax,dataa[si]   ;element from 1st array → ax
              mov      datab[di],al   ;store in 2nd in byte
              inc      di             ;increment destination ind
              inc      si             ;increment source index
              inc      si             ;   in word mode
              loop     l__lp          ;loop till count in cx = 0
    ;
    dataa     dw       10 dup(?)      ;reserve 10 words for dataa
    datab     db       10 dup(?)      ;reserve 10 bytes for datab
```

3. To branch to 8 different locations depending on the bit setting of the accumulator:

```
    Jump to label1 if al  =  00000001
    Jump to label2 if al  =  00000010
    Jump to label3 if al  =  00000100
    Jump to label4 if al  =  00001000
    Jump to label5 if al  =  00010000
    Jump to label6 if al  =  00100000
    Jump to label7 if al  =  01000000
    Jump to label8 if al  =  10000000
    ;
              cmp      ax,0           ;cmp ax with 0
              jz       l__notset      ;jump if equal
```

```
;
        mov     bx,addr__seg        ;address of jump table → bx
        mov     ds,bx               ;       → data seg register
        lea     bx,addr__table      ;offset of addr__table
        mov     si,0                ;source index = 0
        mov     cx,8                ;loop count = 8
;
;       begin main loop
;
l__main: shl    al,1                ;shift highest bit into
                                    ;carry flag
        jnc     l__next             ;jump if bit not set
;
        jmp     word ptr [bx][si]   ;branch to label defined by bx
;
l__next: inc    si                  ;increment source index
        inc     si                  ;   in word mode
        loop    l__main             ;loop till cx = 0
l__notset label near
        ...other processing............................

addr__seg    segment               ;beginning of segment addr__seg
addr__table  dw   label8           ;begining of jump table
             dw   label7
             dw   label6
             dw   label5
             dw   label4
             dw   label3
             dw   label2
             dw   label1            ;end of this jump table
addr__seg    ends                   ;end of this segment
```

4. To copy a character string with NULL terminator:

```
;
;       copy string with null terminator
;       maximum byte = 80
;
        mov     cx,length d__data   ;load cx with max size
        mov     si,0                ;source index = 0
        mov     di,0                ;des index = 0
;
l__20:  mov     al,s__data[si]      ;load s__data → al
        mov     d__data[di],al      ;store al → d__data
        inc     si                  ;next byte
```

```
                inc     di                      ;
                or      al,al                   ;compare al with zero
                loopnz  l__20                   ;repeat loop till
                                                ;cx = 0 or
                                                ;zero flag set
code            ends
;
;               date segment
;
t__data         segment
s__data         db      'source string',0
d__data         db      80 dup(?)
t__data         ends
;
;               output a monthly calendar for 1984
;
;
                extrn   pstg;far
                extrn   pnum:far
                extrn   putc:far
                extrn   pline:far
                extrn   exit:far
LF              equ     0ah
CR              equ     0dh
;
code            segment
                assume cs:code,ds:t__data,ss:stack
go:             mov     ax,t__data
                mov     ds,ax                   ;init ds to t__data
                mov     ax,stack
                mov     ss,ax                   ;init ss to stack
                mov     sp,offset s__data       ;set stack pointer
;
;               output title
;
                mov     dx,offset year          ;load offset of mes
                call    pstg                    ;output question
;
;               main loop for 12 month
;
                mov     cx,12                   ;12 month
                mov     si,0                    ;month address index
                mov     day,1                   ;start from sun
;
;
```

```
l_main:     mov     svmonth,cx              ;save number of month
            mov     dx,month_tbl[si]        ;load offset of heading
            call    pstg                    ;output month
            call    pline
            mov     dx,week
            call    pstg
;
;           output leading spaces for beginning of each month
;
            mov     cx,day                  ;day of 1st in month
            dec     cx
            jcxz    l_weeks
;
            mov     al,' '                  ;load space in al
l sp:       call    putc                    ;output space
            call    putc                    ;output space
            call    putc                    ;output space
            loop    l_sp                    ;repeat for sun,mon...
;
;           output date in month
;
l_weeks:    mov     cx,day_tbl[si]          ;max day of month
            mov     word  ptr  date,1       ;date start from 1st of Jan
;
l_days:     cmp     word  ptr  date,10      ;less than 10, need extra sp
            jge     l_tens
            mov     al,' '                  ;load space in al
            call    putc
;
l_tens:     mov     ax,date
            call    pnum
            mov     al,' '
            call    putc
;
            inc     day
            and     word  ptr  day,7
            jnz     l new
;
;           output new line when Sun.
;
            call    pline
            inc     day                     ;start from 1 again
;
l_new:      inc     date
            loop    l_days
```

```
;
;               end of month, next month?
;
                call    pline
                inc     si
                inc     si
                mov     cx,svmonth              ;retrieve month count
                loop    l__main
;
;               return to msdos
;
                call    exit
code            ends
;
;               data
;
t__data         segment
month__tbl      dw      jan,feb,mar,apr,may,jun
                dw      jul,aug,sep,oct,nov,dec
year            db      '  1 9 8 4',CR,LF,0
week            db      'S M T W T F S        ',CR,LF,0
jan             db      'JANUARY              ',CR,LF,0
feb             db      'FEBRUARY             ',CR,LF,0
mar             db      'MARCH                ',CR,LF,0
apr             db      'APRIL                ',CR,LF,0
may             db      'MAY                  ',CR,LF,0
jun             db      'JUNE                 ',CR,LF,0
jul             db      'JULY                 ',CR,LF,0
aug             db      'AUGUST               ',CR,LF,0
sep             db      'SEPTEMBER            ',CR,LF,0
oct             db      'OCTOBER              ',CR,LF,0
nov             db      'NOVEMBER             ',CR,LF,0
dec             db      'DECEMBER             ',CR,LF,0
day__tbl        db      31,29,31,30,31,30
                db      31,31,30,31,30,31
date            dw      0
day             dw      0
cvmonth         dw      0
t__data         ends
;
stack           segment stack
                db      128 dup(?)
s__data         equ     $
stack           ends
;
                end     go
```

CHAPTER 9

String Manipulation

9.1 STRING INSTRUCTIONS

The 8086-8088 has a set of instructions for performing repetitive operations. Each block instruction eliminates the overheads that are usually required between the processing of successive items.

Each string primitive requires a suffix W or B to specify the size of the operand (word or byte mode).

```
lods        ;Load each string element pointed by ds:si
            ;into the acc.
            ;update si
stos        ;Store the content of the acc into the string
            ;pointed by es:di
            ;update di
movs        ;Move the string pointed to by ds:si
            ;into memory pointed to by es:di
            ;update si, di
cmps        ;compare the elements of two strings
            ;one pointed to by es:di and
            ;the other by ds:si
            ;update si, di
scas        ;Scan a string pointed to by es:di;
            ;comparing each element to the accumulator
            ;and setting the flags to the result of
            ;such a comparison
            ;update di
```

For example:

```
      stosb       ;store the content of al into memory
or    stosw       ;store the content of ax into memory
```

The si, di index registers are updated by 1 for bytes and 2 for words. The adjustment is incremental if the direction flag is 0; otherwise the index registers are decremented:

```
std        ;set the direction flag
cld        ;clear the direction flag
```

A string primitive is used with a loop instruction to complete a repetitive loop sequence of operations. For example:

1. To send 16 words of data starting with crtc to memory map I/O port 0e8000h:

```
              mov     ax,0e000h          ;port address → ax
              mov     es,ax              ;    → extra segment
              mov     si,offset crtc     ;crtc → source index
              mov     cx,16              ;16  → count register
              cld                        ;clear direction flag
;
l__lp:        lodsw                      ;load ax with ds:si
                                         ;& increment source ind
              mov     es:[8000h],ax      ;  → memory mapped address
                                         ; via es
              loop    l__lp              ;loop till cx = 0
```

2. To clear a portion of memory from 2000h for 2000 locations:

```
              mov     ax,200h            ;start address → ax
              mov     es,ax              ; → extra segment reg
              mov     di,0               ;0 → des index
              mov     cx,2000            ;no of locations → cx
              cld                        ;clear df flag
              mov     ax,0               ;clear ax
l__lp:        stosw                      ;es:[di] ← ax
              loop    l__lp              ;loop till cx = 0
```

3. To copy 13 bytes from loc s__data to d__data:

```
              mov     cx,13              ;no of bytes to transfer
              les     di,d__ptr          ;load es,di
              lds     si,s__ptr          ;load ds,si
              cld                        ;clear dir flag
l__20:        movsb                      ;ds:[si] → es:[di]
              loop    l__20              ;loop until cx=0

s__ptr        dd      s__data            ;source pointer
```

```
d__ptr      dd      d__data                 ;des pointer
s__data     db      'source string'         ;source string
d__data     db      13 dup(?)               ;reserve bytes
```

4. Match two character strings:

```
            les     di,d__ptr               ;set up index and segment regs
            lds     si,s__ptr               ;for string instruction
            mov     cx,7                    ;length of test pattern
            cld                             ;clear dir flag si,di increase
1__20:      cmpsb                           ;is ds:[si]=es:[di]
            loope   1__20                   ;repeat while equal
                                            ;or cx not eq 0

            je      1__match                ;jump if equal
;
1__nomatch          label   near
                    ....................
1__match            label   near
                    ....................

;
s__ptr      dd      s__data                 ;dword pointer
d__ptr      dd      d__data                 ;dword pointer
s__data     db      'pattern'               ;test pattern
d__data     db      80 dup(?)               ;fill with data before testing
```

5. Search for '$' within string d__data:

```
            mov     cx,80                   ;max string length
            les     di,d__ptr               ;load es:di
            mov     al,'$'                  ;'$' → al
1__40:      scasb                           ;compare with al
            loopnz  1__40                   ;loop until cx=0
                                            ;or zero flag set

            je      1__found                ;jump if [di] = al
;
1__nofound          label   near
                    ....................
1__found            label   near
                    ....................

;
d__ptr      dd      d__data
d__data     db      'string for the test$'
```

Repeat Prefix

The rep prefix causes a succeeding string operation to be repeated until the count in cx goes to zero (rep causes cx to be decremented after each repetition of the string operation). If the string operation is either scas or cmps, then the zf is compared to the repeat condition after the string operation is performed, and the instruction is terminated if the zf does not match the condition.

```
rep              ;repeat next instruction until cx=0
repe             ;repeat next instruction until
                 ;cx = 0 or zf = 1
repz             ;same as repe
repne            ;repeat next instruction until
                 ;cx = 0 or zf = 0
repnz            ;same as repne
```

For example:

1. To clear a portion of memory from address 2000h for 2000 locations:

```
mov     ax,200h          ;start addres → ax
mov     es,ax            ;   → extra seg reg
mov     di,0             ;0 → des index reg
mov     cx,2000          ;2000 → count register
cld                      ;clear df flag
mov     ax,0             ;clear ax
rep     stosw            ;repeat store es:di = ax
                         ;& inc di till cx = 0
```

2. To compare two ASCII character strings:

```
mov     di,offset buffer         ;addr of string → di
mov     si,offset test__string   ;addr test string → si
mov     cx,8                     ;string length → cx
cld                              ;clear direction flag
repe    cmpsb                    ;cont compare bytes
je      l__match                 ;jump if found a match
jg      l__great                 ;test > buffer
;
l__less  label    near           ;test < buffer
```

3.

```
;
;          to use the string instruction for screen display
;

extrn   exit:far         ;exit to msdos
extrn   clr:far          ;clear screen
```

```
;
code        segment
            assume  cs:code,ds:t__data,ss:stack
;
;           init segment registers
;
go:         mov     ax,t__data
            mov     ds,ax                   ;data segment
            mov     ax,stack
            mov     ss,ax                   ;init ss to stack
            mov     sp,offset s__data       ;set stack pointer

;
;           clear screen
;
            call    clr                     ;clear screen
;
;   display characters
;
            mov     ax,0f000h               ;load base of screen address
            mov     es,ax                   ;extra segments register = 0f000h
;
            mov     si,offset name__a       ;address of name__a→ si
            mov     di,0                    ;0→ di
            mov     cx,3                    ;no of characters in string
            rep     movsw                   ;string move
;           return to msdos
            call    exit
code        ends
;
;           data area
;
t__data     segment
name__a     db      'A'+64h,80h             ;inverse video
name__c     dw      'C'+100+40h*256         ;half intensity
name__t     db      'T'+100                 ;underline
t__data     ends
;
stack       segment  stack
            db      128 dup(?)
s__data     equ     $
stack       ends
;
            end     go
```

9.2 TABLE LOOKUP

XLAT is intended for use as a table lookup instruction. The base address of the table is stored in reg bx, and a byte to be translated in al. XLAT adds al to the contents of bx and uses the result as an effective address. The byte at that ea is loaded into al. bx is unchanged, and no flags are modified.

```
xlat     ;al = [bx+al], 11 clock cycle
```

Apart from the saving time and bx remaining unchanged, xlat is equivalent to:

```
cbw                ;al → ax
add   bx,ax        ;modify address
mov   al,[bx]      ;load ax, total of 15 clock cycles
```

For example:

1. To translate ASCII to EBCDIC, load a conversion table for the ASCII to EBCDIC using define directives (db) then convert a string of numbers from ASCII to EBCDIC (Figure 9.1):

```
          mov   bx,offset table      ;beginning of table
          mov   cx,8
          lds   si,n__ptr            ;pointer to ASCII String
          les   di,bcd__ptr          ;pointer to EBCDIC string
l__00:    lodsb                      ;ds:[si] → al, inc si
          xlat                       ;al → [bx+al]
          stosb                      ;al → es:[di], inc di
          loopl__00                  ;repeat till cx count
                                     ;= zero
```

2. In Chapter 7, a menu-driven program with options 0,1,2,3,... was given as an example of unconditional branching. A number of programs also use single-character commands, i.e.

```
E  – exit
T  – transmit
R  – receive
D  – directory, etc.
```

After reading the command character from the keyboard, the program can compare it with each valid letter and branch accordingly. If the command character is loaded in al:

```
          cmp   al,'E'
          jne   l2
```

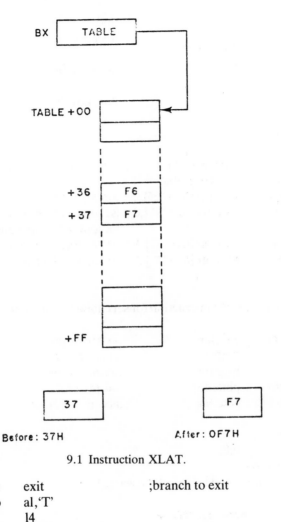

9.1 Instruction XLAT.

```
        jmp     exit                ;branch to exit
l2:     cmp     al,'T'
        jne     l4
        jmp     transmit            ;branch to transmit
l4:     cmp     al,'R'
        je      receive             ;branch to receive
        ..........etc ......
```

Alternatively, one can translate the character into a number 0–3, and use a jump table to branch to each of the processing routines as described in Chapter 7.

The table for xlat can be set up in two ways:

1. at assemble time:

```
    table   db          −1,−1,...
```

```
                3                      ;location 'D'
                0                      ;location 'E'
                -1,-1...
                2                      ;location 'R'
                -1
                1                      ;location 'T'
```

2. at run time:

```
  table   db      128 dup (-1)            ;set up table with -1
          mov     bx,offset table
          mov     byte ptr [bx+'E'],0    ;set up location table+'E' with 0
          mov     byte ptr [bx+'e'],0    ;set up location table+'e' with 0
                                         ;accept both upper and lower case
          mov     byte ptr [bx+'T'],1    ;set up location table+'T' with 1
          mov     byte ptr [bx+'t'],1    ;set up location table+'t' with 1
          ...... etc ......
;
;               To use the xlat instruction for set character attribute
;
          extrn   exit:far               ;exit to msdos
          extrn   clr:far                ;clear screen
          extrn   pstg:far               ;output string
          extrn   pline:far              ;output cr,lf
          extrn   getc:far               ;accept a character
;
CR        equ     0ah
LF        equ     0dh
code        segment
            assume cs:code,ds:t__data,ss:stack
;
;               init segment registers
;
go:       mov     ax,t__data
          mov     ds,ax                  ;data segment
          mov     ax,stack
          mov     ss,ax                  ;init ss to stack
          mov     sp,offset   s__data    ;set stack pointer
;
;               load table of attribute
;
          mov     bx,offset OPTBL
          mov     byte ptr [bx+'N'],11100000b
          mov     byte ptr [bx+'n'],11100000b
          mov     byte ptr [bx+'I'],10000000b
```

```
        mov     byte ptr [bx + 'i'  ],10000000b
        mov     byte ptr [bx + 'H'],01000000b
        mov     byte ptr [bx + 'h' ],01000000b
        mov     byte ptr [bx + 'U'],00100000b
        mov     byte ptr [bx + 'u' ],00100000b
        mov     byte ptr [bx + 'R'],00000000b
        mov     byte ptr [bx + 'r' ],00000000b
;
;       clear screen
;
        call    clr                         ;clear screen
;
;       get screen attribute
;
        mov     dx,offset menu0
        call    pstg
l__attr: mov    dx,offset prompt
        call    pstg
        call    getc
        mov     bx,optbl
        xlat
        cmp     al,-1
        jne     l__attr
        mov     attb,al
;
;       display characters
;
        mov     ax,0f000h                   ;load base of screen address
        mov     es,ax                       ;extra segment register = 0f000h
;
        mov     si,offset name__stg         ;address of name__a → si
        mov     di,0                        ;0 → di
        mov     ah,attb
;
;       main loop terminate at null
;
l__disp: lodsb
        cmp     al,0                        ;null character?
        je      l__exit
        add     al,100                      ;font table offset
        stosw                               ;move to screen includes attr.
        jmp     l__disp
;
;       return to msdos
l__exit: call   exit
```

106

```
code        ends
;
;           data area
;
t__data     segment
name__stg   db          'ACT',0
attb        db          0
optbl       db          256 dup(-1)
menu0       db          ' [N]ormal',CR,LF
            db          ' [U]nderline',CR,LF
            db          ' [I]nverse',CR,LF
            db          ' [H]alf intensity',CR,LF
            db          ' [R]eset'CR,LF,LF,LF,0
prompt      db          'enter option   ',0
t__data     ends
;
stack       segement stack
            db          128 dup(?)
s__data     equ         $
stack       ends
;
            end         go
```

CHAPTER 10

Subprogramming Concept

10.1 PROCEDURE

When the same sequence of instructions is required to be performed a number of times in various parts of a program, these instructions should be defined as a procedure:

```
name      proc      ⟨type⟩

name      endp
```

where ⟨type⟩ may be either near or far (default to near if not specified). This defines the length of the return instruction, i.e. near = 2 bytes, far = 4 bytes.

Each program is therefore divided into a main module and one or more procedures, in one or more source files. The main module jumps to the beginning of a procedure by executing a CALL instruction. The last instruction the procedure executes is a RET instruction, such that the program returns to the next sequential instruction following the call. This operation can be repeated as often as required without greatly increasing the size of the program. Procedure calls can also be nested:

```
call   name     ;execute proc name
ret             ;return
ret    nn       ;return and clear nn locations in stack
```

Procedure Parameters

When calling a procedure, it is very often necessary to pass several parameters (variables) to the routine. General registers can be used in two different ways, provided the parameter's value is small and there are only a few of them.

Pass by value – the contents of variables are loaded into the general reg before passing.

For example:

> putc :– output a character to console

To output a character, load reg al with the character required and execute the routine putc.

```
;
;          The ACT display control code for clear sceen is esc 'E'
;
           mov    al,esc              ;ascii value of esc → al
           call   putc                ;o/p the char in al
           mov    al,'E'              ;'E' → al
           call   putc                ;o/p the char in al
```

Values can also be returned in predefined registers. For example:

> gnum :– accept a number from the keyboard

```
           call   gnum                ;await a char at the keyboard
           mov    num,ax              ;integer return in ax
num        dw     0
```

Pass by address – the offsets of variables are loaded into the general reg before passing. An extra step is required to access the content of the variables, but provides a means of updating the variables within the procedure

For example:

> pstg :– output a string of characters

To output a string of characters, load dx with the address of the first character of the string terminated by null.

```
           mov    dx,offset message            ;addr of o/p string → dx
           call   pstg                         ;o/p string
message    db     'this is the message',0
;
;          procedure pstg
;
pstg       proc   near
;
;          procedure name :– pstg
;
```

```
;              function – output a string of characters to console
;                            string terminates by null.;
               entry
;              dx – address of first byte of string
;
l__nextc:  mov    bx,dx          ;dx → bx
           mov    al,[bx]        ;byte address by bx → al
           cmp    al,0           ;if = null then
           je     lstg           ;end of o/p
;
           call   putc           ;output char in al
           inc    bx             ;increment byte pointer
           jmp    l__nextc       ;jump to o/p next byte
;
lstg:      ret                   ;return to calling routine
pstg       endp                  ;end of this procedure
```

10.2 STACK

A last-in/first-out (LIFO) stack is maintained by the 8086/8088 processor under software control. The stack provides an orderly method of storing a procedure return address and return from a procedure. A return address is saved on the stack automatically when a procedure call is executed. If the name of the procedure is defined with type far, then four bytes containing both the instruction pointer ip and the code segment address are pushed on the stack. With a procedure within the same segment, i.e. name proc near, only the ip is pushed on the stack.

The stack facility provides not only the return address for a procedure call, but also an expandable area of temporary storage for variables and registers. The same stack can be used for passing the procedure's parameters.

Stack Manipulation Instructions

```
push   mem16           ;push a word on stack
push   reg16           ;push general register on stack
push   segreg          ;push segment register on stack
pushf                  ;push flags on stack

pop    mem16           ;pop a word from stack
pop    reg16           ;pop general register from stack
pop    segreg          ;pop segment register from stack
popf                   ;pop flags from stack

mov    sp, offset name ;set up a local stck
```

Use of a LIFO stack

Listed below is a procedure that outputs decimal numbers. In order to display a number, say 124, then split the number into two parts using the idiv instruction:

124 divided by 10 → remainder 4
124 divided by 10 → quotient 12.

The digit 4 can easily be converted into a character code and output by putc. The process can be repeated on the quotient part. Unfortunately, this produces the digits in the reverse order.

However, this difficulty can be averted neatly by using the LIFO stack. Each digit is pushed on the stack when calculated. When the quotient is zero, each digit is retrieved from the stack and converted into character code for printing.

The listing of such a procedure is as follows,

```
pnum            proc    far              ;define pnum for general use
;
;           procedure name :- pnum
;
;           function :-  To output an integer number in ASCII with leading
;                        zero suppressed.
;
;           entry :-
;           ax - integer
;           external procedures required        :- putc
;
                push    ax               ;save
                push    bx               ;  all
                push    cx               ;    general
                push    dx               ;      registers
;
;           check sign of number
;
                mov     cx,0             ;clear counter
                cmp     ax,0             ;if a >= 0
                jge     l__ndigit        ;   then jump to l__ndigit
;
;           number negative, output a '-' sign
;
                push    ax               ;save ax on stack
                mov     al,'-'           ;'-' → al
                call    putc             ;output content of al
                pop     ax               ;restore ax from stack
                neg     ax               ;complement it
```

```
;
;               process number
;
l__ndigit:      cwd                      ;convert to double word
                mov      bx,10           ;load bx with 10
                div      bx              ;dx:ax/10
;
                push     dx              ;save remainder on stack
                inc      cx              ;increment count register
                cmp      ax,0            ;if quotient = 0
                jnz      l__ndigit       ;next digit
;
l__nout:        pop      ax              ;retrieve digit from stack
                add      al,'0'          ;convert to ascii
                call     putc            ;output content of al
                loop     l__nout         ;cont till cont in cx = 0
                pop      dx              ;restore
                pop      cx              ;        all the
                pop      bx              ;              registers
                pop      ax              ;               from stack
                ret                      ;exit to calling routine
pnum            endp                     ;end of this procedure
```

Parameters passed via the stack

Besides the passing of parameters via registers and memory, a third possibility
is to pass the parameters on the stack and have the procedure access the stack.
This is the most common method used by high-level languages (Figure 10.1).

To access the parameters, one uses the bp register plus a displacement value
defined by the procedure. As shown in the figure, the return address is at
bp+4, and the parameters are at bp+6, bp+8,... .

Another benefit of using the stack is that after copying sp into bp, values can
be subtracted from the stack pointer. Using a negative displacement with bp,
one can reserve and access this area as a workspace for the procedure's local
variables, giving the procedure the ability to use it as a re-entrant routine

```
proc__0    proc near
;
;          module name :- proc__0
;
;          function :- To show how parameters and local variables
;                      on stack can be defined and accessed.
;
;          external procedures required :- none
;
```

112

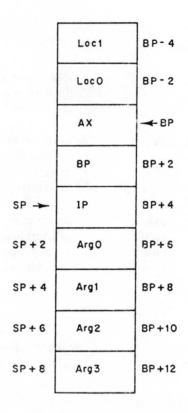

10.1 Parameters passed via the STACK.

```
;
;           on entry :-
;           sp+8        -arg 3
;           sp+6        -arg 2
;           sp+4        -arg 1
;           sp+2        -arg 0
;           sp          - return offset address
;
;           define arguments on stack
;           reg bp, ax are saved
i__arg0     equ         word ptr [bp+6]
i__arg1     equ         word ptr [bp+8]
i__arg2     equ         word ptr [bp+10]
i__arg3     equ         word ptr [bp+12]
;
;           define local variables
;
i__loc0     equ         word ptr [bp-2]
i__loc1     equ         word ptr [bp-4]
;
```

```
;          save all general and segment registers used
;
;          push    bp              ;save bp
           push    ax              ;all
;
;          local variables on stack
;
           mov     bp,sp           ;store stack pointer → bp
           sub     sp,4            ;sp = last local variable
;
;          retrieve arguments on stack
;
           mov     ax,i__arg1      ;accessing variables on stack
           .... process ....
;
;          return control to calling program
;
           mov     sp,bp           ;restore stack pointer
           pop     ax              ;          registers
           pop     bp              ;          from stack
;
           ret     8               ;ret & clear locations used by args
proc__0    endp                    ;end of this procedure
```

To call the procedure, the argument list are pushed on the stack in the reverse order:

```
           push    arg3
           push    arg2
           push    arg1
           push    arg0
           call    proc__0
```

Procedures defined as far:

```
draw__arc proc     far
;
;          module name    :−  draw__arc
;
;
;          function       :−  This procedure joints the two co-ord pairs
;                             with an arc at centre xc,yc
;
;
;          external procedures required :−  dpixel
;
;          on entry       :−
;          sp+14              −  final y co-ord
```

```
;              sp+12         − final x co-ord
;              sp+10         − initial y co-ord
;              sp+8          − initial x co-ord
;              sp+6          − y centre
;              sp+4          − x centre
;              sp,sp+2       − return address
;
;         define arguments on stack
;
xc            equ       word ptr [bp+14]
yc            equ       word ptr [bp+16]
ixc           equ       word ptr [bp+18]
iyc           equ       word ptr [bp+20]
fxc           equ       word ptr [bp+22]
fyc           equ       word ptr [bp+24]
;
;         define locals on stacks
;
t__dir        equ       word ptr [bp−2]
t__dir1       equ       word ptr [bp−4]
t__syfinal    equ       word ptr [bp−6]
t__z          equ       word ptr [bp−8]
t__z1         equ       word ptr [bp−10]
t__z2         equ       word ptr [bp−12]
t__dir2       equ       word ptr [bp−14]
;
;         save all general and segment registers used
;              push      bp           ;save bp
                push      ax           ;all
                push      bx           ;   general
                push      cx           ;      registers
                push      dx           ;         used
;
;         decrease stack pointer for nested procedure calls
;
                mov       bp,sp        ;store stack pointer → bp
                sub       sp,14        ;sp = last local variable
;
;         retrieve arguments on stack
;
                mov       bx,iyc
                mov       dx,ixc
;
;         begin processing
;

                     ......................
```

```
;
;              return control to calling program
;
               mov    sp,bp
               pop    dx        ;restore
               pop    cx        ;        all
               pop    bx        ;            the
               pop    ax        ;              registers
               pop    bp        ;                from stack
;
               ret    12        ;ret & clear locations used by args
draw arc       endp             ;end of this procedure
;
;
;              to call the above procedure to draw a circle
;              the initial co-ord and the final co-ord of the
;              draw__arc procedure is set to be equal
;
;              call drawarc(xc,yc,0,radius,0,radius)
;
;              the input parameters can be set as follows
;
               mov    ax,0      ;clear ax
               push   radius
               push   ax        ;put on stack
               push   radius
               push   ax        ;push on stack
               push   yc
               push   xc
               call   draw__arc ;call procedure draw__arc
;
;
;              example of a procedure with four parameters
;
;                  1. x co-ord on the screen (0–79)
;                  2. y co-ord on the screen (0–23)
;                  3. offset address of the text string
;                  4. character attribute code
;                     H – half intensity
;                     I – inverse video
;                     U – underlined
;
;              Write a main program using a separate source file
;              to test your procedure.
;
```

116

```
            extrn   exit:far                ;exit to msdos
            extrn   clr:far                 ;clear screen
            extrn   gnum:far                ;input an integer
            extrn   getc:far                ;input a char
            extrn   pstg:far                ;output a char string
            extrn   position:far            ;output string
;
main        segment
            assume cs:main,ds:main,ss:stack
;
;           init segment registers
;
go:         mov     ax,main
            mov     ds,ax                   ;data segment
            mov     ax,stack
            mov     ss,ax                   ;init ss to stack
            mov     sp,offset s__data       ;set stack pointer
;
;           clear screen
;
            call    clr                     ;clear screen
;
;           operator prompts
;
            mov     dx,offset mes1          ;address of mes1 → dx
            call    pstg                    ;display message
            call    gnum                    ;read x co-ord
            mov     xc,ax                   ;x co-ord → xc
;
            mov     dx,offset mes2          ;address of mes2 → dx
            call    pstg                    ;display message
            call    gnum                    ;read y co-ord
            mov     yc,ax                   ;y co-ord → yc
;
            mov     dx,offset mes3          ;address of mes3 → dx
            call    pstg                    ;display message
            call    getc                    ;read attribute
            mov     att,ax                  ;attr. → att
;
;           display characters
;
            push    att                     ;passing
            push    ds                      ;   parameters
            mov     ax,offset mes4          ;via
            push    ax                      ;   stack
```

```
            push    yc
            push    xc
            call    position            ;display ACT
;
;           return to msdos
            call    exit
;
;           data area
;
xc          dw      0
yc          dw      0
att         dw      0
mes1        db      'enter x co-ord   ',0
mes2        db      'enter y co-ord   ',0
mes3        db      'enter char attribute   ',0
mes4        db      'ACT SIRIUS',0
main        ends
;
stack       segment   stack
            db      256 dup(?)
s__data     equ     $
stack       ends
;
            end     go
```

In a separate source file, the procedure is defined:

```
;
;
            extrn   pstg:far            ;output a char string
            public  position            ;procedure to output char
code        segment
            assume  cs:code
;
;           define procedure
;
position        proc        far
;
;           on entry    :–
;           sp+12       – character attribute
;           sp+10       – segment address of the text string
;           sp+8        – offset address of the text string
;           sp+6        – y co-ord on the screen
;           sp+4        – x co-ord on the screen
;           sp,sp+2     – return address
```

```
;
;               define arguments on stack
;
xc        equ       word ptr [bp+16]
yc        equ       word ptr [bp+18]
mes       equ       dword ptr [bp+20]
char__at  equ       byte ptr [bp+24]
;
;               save registers
;
          push      bp                  ;save
          push      ds                  ;   all
          push      ax                  ;       registers
          push      bx
          push      cx
          push      dx
          mov       bp,sp               ;bp points to base
;
;               display characters
;
          mov       ax,0f000h           ;load base of screen address
          mov       es,ax               ;0f000h→es
;
;               calculate start address on screen
;
;               base = y * 160 + x * 2
;
          mov       ax,yc               ;yc→ ax
          mov       cx,160              ;160→ cx
          imul      cx                  ;y * 160→ dx:ax
          mov       bx,xc               ;xc→ bx
          add       bx,bx               ;2 * xc→ bx
          add       bx,ax               ;screen offset → bx
;
;               check character attribute
;
          mov       ah,0                ;clear ah
          mov       al,char__at         ;attribute → al
          cmp       al,'I'              ;is attr = inverse
          jnz       l__0                ;skip not equal
          mov       ah,80h              ;set inverse video attr.
          jmp       l__begin            ;branch to display
l__0:     cmp       al,'H'              ;is attr = half intensity
          jnz       l__2                ;skip not equal
          mov       ah,40h              ;set half int. attr.
```

```
         jmp    l__begin        ;branch to display
l__2:    cmp    al,'U'          ;is attr = underline
         jnz    l__begin        ;non of the above,
                                ;default to normal
         mov    ah,20h          ;set underline attr.
;
;              display character string
;
l__begin: lds   si,mes          ;start message addr → si
l__next: mov    al,ds:[si]      ;load char from string
         cmp    al,0            ;null char is string terminator
         jz     quit            ;exit loop
;
         add    al,100          ;required by act screen
         mov    es:[bx],ax      ;display on screen
         inc    bx              ;next screen character
         inc    bx              ;position
         inc    si              ;next message character
         jmp    l__next         ;repeat until end of string
;
;              return to msdos
;
;
quit:    mov    sp,bp           ;retrieve
         pop    dx              ;   all
         pop    cx              ;registers
         pop    bx
         pop    ax
         pop    ds
         pop    bp
         ret    10              ;return to main module with
                                ;stack pop (5 parameters)
position endp                   ;end of procedure
;
code     ends                   ;end of segment
         end                    ;end of source module
```

To link the program, use

LINK MAIN+POSITION+STDIO;

CHAPTER 11

Direct Input/Output

I/O devices may be addressed like memory devices and mov instructions used to transfer data to and from them (see Section 4.4). This reduces the available amount of memory space for the user programs.

There are two input/output instructions for the 8086/8088 processor, giving their own special addressing space separate from the memory. Sections 11.1 and 11.2 describe the I/O instructions.

In Section 11.3, both the 8086 hardware and software interrupts are examined.

11.1 IN INSTRUCTION

Direct	in	al,port__number	;port data → al
	in	ax,port__number	;port data → ax
Indirect	in	al,dx	;port specified by dx → al
	in	ax,dx	;port specified by dx → ax

The IN instruction transfers a byte or word from the specified input port to al or ax. Use of the direct instruction format spcifies a 1-byte port address allowing access to port 0 through 0ffh, and encodes the port number in the instruction. To use the indirect instruction format, dx has to be loaded with a 16-bit port number, thus allowing access to 64K ports. The ability to manipulate register dx enables programs to be read from several I/O ports. For example, to input a block of data:

	mov	cx,loop__count	;loop__count → cx
l__next:	in	al,port	;input port → al
	stosb		;al → es:di, di+1 → di
	loop	l__next	;dec cx & loop till cx = 0

120

11.2 OUT INSTRUCTION

```
out   port_number,al      ;al → port
out   port_number,ax      ;ax → port

out   dx,al               ;al → port specified by dx
out   dx,ax               ;ax → port specified by dx
```

The out instruction transfers a byte or word from the specified output port to al or ax. Use of the direct instruction format specifies a 1-byte port address allowing access to port 0 through 0ffh, and encodes the port number in the instruction. To use the indirect instruction format, dx has to be loaded with a 16-bit port number, thus allowing access to 64K ports. The ability to manipulate register dx enables programs to communicate with several I/O ports. For example, to output a block of data:

```
          mov   cx,loop_count      ;loop_count → cx
l_next:   lodsb                    ;ds:[si] → al
          out   port,al            ;al → output port
          loop  l_next             ;dec c & loop till cx = 0
```

11.3 INTERRUPTS

The 8086 has several sources of interrupts. An interrupt can come from external devices or software instructions.

Hardware Interrupts

External devices can set the two lines in the 8086/8088 to signal interrupts: interrupt input INTR (interrupt request), or NMI (nonmaskable interrupt). The INTR line is driven by an 8259 programmable interrupt controller. The CPU examines the interrupt input at the end of each instruction cycle and causes the process to execute an interrupt service routine (ISR) if the interrupt-enable flag is set. The 8086/8088 executes in a vectored interrupt mode. The I/O device controller provides both the interrupt and an 8-bit value identifying the device. This number is known as the interrupt type.

The address of each ISR is stored in a 256-entry table, beginning at location 0. Each table entry is four bytes long, containing the values of cs and ip of each ISR.

A nonmaskable interrupt (NMI) request can arrive on another CPU line from an external source. This line signals to the CPU that a catastrophic event—such as the imminent loss of power, or a memory error detection—has occurred. Interrupt requests arriving on NMI cannot be disabled. NMIs are predefined as type 2.

Software Interrupts

Execution of an interrupt (INT) instruction generates an immediate interrupt. The interrupt type code identifies the procedure needed to process the interrupt:

```
int  n                    ;software interrupt
into                      ;interrupt on overflow
iret                      ;interreupt return
```

int n, into pushes the flag registers, clears both the interrupt and trap flags, and transfers control with an indirect call through any one of the 256 elements in the interrupt pointer table. Each interrupt routine returns with an IRET instruction.

There are a number of reserved interrupt types:

```
int  0                    ;divided by zero
int  1                    ;single stepping for debug
int  2                    ;NMI interrupt
int  3                    ;1 byte int instruction
int  4                    ;signed overflow
int  5–int 31             ;reserved for future expansion
                          ;by Intel
```

INT n is also used in communication with the operating system (supervisor call) for other programs in the system (Table 11.1).

INTO pushes the flag registers, and transfers control with an indirect call through vector element 4 (location 10h) if the overflow flag is set (trap on overflow).

IRET returns control to an interrupted routine by transferring control to the return address saved by a previous interrupt operation and restoring the saved flag registers (as in POPF).

Interrupt Flags

The 8086 processor has two control flags, interrupt-enable flag and trap flag in the flag register. The STI (CLI) enable (disable) all external maskable interrupts:

```
sti                     ;set interrupt-enable flag
cli                     ;clear interrupt-enable flag
```

Table 11.1   Interrupt pointers.

3ffh	Type 255 pointer	
	....	available
		interrupt
080h	Type 32 pointer	pointers
07fh		
	Type 31 pointer	
	....	reserved
		interrupt
014h	Type 5 pointer	pointers
010h	Type 4 pointer	
	signed overflow	
00ch	Type 3 pointer	
	1 byte INT inst.	
008h	Type 2 pointer	
	Non-Maskable	
004h	Type 1 pointer	
	single step	
		dedicated
000h	Type 0 pointer	interrupt
	divide by zero	pointers

When the trap flag is set, the processor generates a int 1 interrupt after the execution of each instruction. This allows a diagnostic task to single-step through a task under test, while still executing normally itself.

No instructions are provided for setting and clearing the trap flag directly. It can be set by modifying the flag register:

```
pushf
pop     ax          ;flag → ax
or      ax,0100h     ;set trap flag
push    ax
popf                 ;ax → flag
```

To clear the flag:

```
pushf
pop     ax              ;flag
and     ax,0feffh       ;clear trap flag
push    ax
popf                    ;ax → flag
```

CHAPTER 12

More Data Types

In addition to the standard data types defined in Chapter 3, the macro assembler allows other structure data types to be defined. A structured data type is defined in terms of one or more previously defined data types, using a structured method.

When storage space is at a premium, it may be necessary to pack several objects into a single byte/word. A record is a set of adjacent bits within a single byte/word. The syntax of record definition and access is described in Section 12.1.

A structure data type is a collection of one or more variables, possibly of different types, grouped together under a single name for convenient handling. (STRUC is identical to both PASCAL 'RECORD' and the C programming language 'STRUCTURE' type.)

12.1 RECORD

⟨recordname⟩　record　⟨fieldname⟩:⟨width⟩[=⟨exp⟩]..[..]

RECORD defines individual fields of n bits in ⟨recordname⟩.
⟨recordname⟩ − name of record definition
⟨fieldname⟩ − the name of the field.
⟨width⟩ − specifies the number of bits in the field, range from 1 to 16.
⟨exp⟩ − contains the initial value for the field.

The first field declared goes into the most significant bits of the record. Successively declared fields are placed in the succeeding bits to the right. If the fields declared do not total exactly 8 bits or 16 bits, the entire record is right shifted so that the last bit of the last field is the lowest bit of the record. Unused bits will be in the high end of the record. For example:

　　drec　　record　　high:4,mid:3,low:3

Total number of its = 4 + 3 + 3 = 12, thus

drec =

```
0 1 2 3 4 5 6 7 8 9  a b c d e f
- - - - - - - h i g h m i d l o w        ;most significant bits
                                          ;are not used
```

To initialize records, use the same method used for define.

[⟨name⟩]   ⟨recordname⟩   ⟨[exp⟩ [,...]⟩

or

[⟨name⟩]   ⟨recordname⟩   [⟨exp⟩ dup(⟨exp][,..]⟩)

⟨name⟩ is a label for the first byte (word) of the record storage area. For example, in

mrec   drec   ⟨0ah,3,5⟩

the name of the record is mrec with type defined by drec. The contents are:

high = 0ah
mid   = 3
low   = 5

```
0 1 2 3 4 5 6 7 8 9 a b c d e f
- - - - - - 1 0 1 0 0 1 1 1 0 1
```

Field Operators

To isolate one record field, specific operators are operated on the record:

1. Shift count
2. Width
3. Mask

Shift count

This gives the number of bits the field must be right shifted in order to right justify the bits in a location:

```
;
;          to extract the field high from the record drec
;
          mov   dx,mrec      ;record mrec → dx
          mov   cl,high      ;shift count operator = rec name
```

```
                              ;bits to be shifted → cl = 6
       shr     dx,cl          ;right justified the bits
```

Width

This returns the width of a field in a record. For example:

```
       mov    cl,width mid    ;width of mid → cl = 3
       mov    ch,width high   ;width of high → ch = 4
```

Mask

This returns a bit-mask for bit positions occupied by the field. For example:

```
   mov    dx,mask mid     ;bits for the field mid are turned
                          ;to 1 else to 0
                          ;i.e. dx = 00 000 000 00 111 000

   mov    ax,not mask mid ;bits for the field mid are turned
                          ;to 0 else to 1
                          ;i.e. ax = 11 111 111 11 000 111
```

```
;
;          To declare record date, and define drec with initial
;          values,
date       record month:4, day:5, year:7      ;declare record 'date'
birthday   .date  ⟨12,25,83⟩                  ;define drec
                                              ;record type = date
                                              ;initial values
                                              ;month = 12
                                              ;day = 25
                                              ;year = 83
```

```
;
;          To store ax in record field.month
;
           mov    dx,birthday       ;record date → dx
           mov    bx,mask month     ;set the month field to 1s
           not    bx                ;complement bx
           and    dx,bx             ;clear month field
           mov    cl,month          ;shift count
           shl    ax,cl             ;shift ax in place with month__field
           or     dx,ax             ;set the field with existing record
           mov    birthday,dx       ;store the record in birthday
```

If birthday = ⟨12,25,83⟩ and ax = 10, the contents of registers after these instructions are:

```
                                              [0 1 2 3 4 5 6 7 8 9 a b c d e f]
                                        ax: 0 0 0 0 0 0 0 0 0 0 0 1 0 1 0
mov   dx,birthday                       dx:   1 1 0 0 1 1 0 0 1 1 0 1 0 0 1 1
mov   bx,mask month                     bx:   1 1 1 1 0 0 0 0 0 0 0 0 0 0
not   bx                                bx: 0 0 0 0 1 1 1 1 1 1 1 1 1 1 1 1
and   dx,bx                             dx: 0 0 0 0 1 1 0 0 1 1 0 1 0 0 1 1
mov   cl,month                          cl:                   0 0 0 0 1 1 0 0
shl   ax,cl                             ax: 1 0 1 0 0 0 0 0 0 0 0 0 0 0 0 0
or    dx,ax                             dx: 1 0 1 0 1 1 0 0 1 1 0 1 0 0 1 1
```

Note that
```
    mov   bx,mnask month
    not   bx
    and   dx,bx
```

is equivalent to

```
    and   dx,not mask month
```

```
;
;              To compare month field with ax
;              extract the field–month then compare with ax
;
;
;              mov   dx,birthday       ;dx = date of month
               and   dx,mask month     ;month → dx,other fields = 0
               mov   cl,month          ;shift count → cl
               shr   dx,cl             ;dx = month
               cmp   ax,dx             ;if(this month = month field)
               jne   l__not__eq
               .................................
```

If birthday = ⟨12,25,83⟩ and ax = 10, the contents of the registers after these instructions are:

```
                                              [0 1 2 3 4 5 6 7 8 9 a b c d e f]
                                        ax: 0 0 0 0 0 0 0 0 0 0 0 1 0 1 0
mov   dx,birthday                       dx:   1 1 0 0 1 1 0 0 1 1 0 1 0 0 1 1
and   dx,mask month                     dx:   1 1 0 0 0 0 0 0 0 0 0 0 0 0 0 0
```

```
mov    cl,month                          cl:              00001100
shr    dx,cl                             dx: 0000000000001100
```

```
;
;              This program tests for the field  –  month in record
;
;
;
;              record definition
;
date          record    month:4,day:5,year:7
;
;              await month entry at the keyboard
;
l__start:     mov    dx,offset msg__month        ;addr of o/p string → dx
              call   pstg                        ;display the string
              call   gnum                        ;await for no. at keyboard
              cmp    al,12                        ;if entry > 12
              jg     l__start                     ;   start again
              cmp    al,0                         ;if entry < 0
              jle    l__start                     ;   start again
;
;              store this in record month__field
;
              mov    dx,birthday                 ;addr of record → dx
              and    dx,not mask month           ;clear month__field
              mov    cl,month                    ;set the mask for the month &
              shl    ax,cl                        ;move to the correct position
              or     dx,ax                        ;dx=month set in the record
              mov    birthday,dx                 ;update drec
;
;              await this month at the keyboard
;
l__2:         mov    dx,offset msg__month1;       addr of o/p string → dx
              call   pstg                        ;o/p the string
              call   gnum                        ;await for no at keyboard
              cmp    ax,0                         ;if < 0 input again
              jz     l__2
;
;              compare the keyboard entry with month__field
;
              mov    dx,birthday                 ;record drec → dx
              and    dx,mask month               ;extract month__field → dx
              mov    cl,month                    ;bits to be shifted → cl
              shr    dx,cl                        ;right justify the field
```

```
;
            cmp     dx,ax                   ;comp dx and ax
            jne     l_2                     ;if no equal jump to l_2
;
            mov     dx,offset ms1           ;addr of message to display → dx
            call    pstg                    ;o/p the message
            jmp     l_start
;
;           data area
;
msg_month   db      'enter month of birth',0
msg_month1  db      'enter this month',0
ms1         db      'it's your birthday this month',0ah,0dh,0
;
;           record definition
;
birthday  date    ⟨7,28,51⟩                ;record with 3 fields
                                            ;1st field = 7
                                            ;2nd = 28, 3rd = 51
```

12.2 STRUCTURE

⟨structure_name⟩   struc
                            .
                            .
⟨structure_name⟩   ends

The struc directive is very much like record except struc defines each field in multiple bytes. For example:

```
            birthday    struc
            date        db   0      ;date with 1 byte
            month       db   0      ;month with 1 byte
            year        db   0      ;year with 1 byte
            birthday    ends        ;end of definition
```

The initial values given to fieldnames in the struc/ends block are default values for the various fields. These values of the fields are one of two types:

1. Overridable – a simple field, a field with only one entry (but not a dup expression).
   – a string, may be overridden by another string. However, if the overriding string is shorter than the initial string, the assembler will pad with spaces. If the overriding string is longer, the assembler will truncate the extra characters.
2. Not overridable – a multiple field.

For example:

```
student    struct
name       db   'TOM'
           db   0
address    db   'LONDON',0
age        db   15
birth      db   25,12,83
marks      dw   10 dup(0)
student    ends
```

Fields name and age are overridable because they are single-entry fields; fields address, birth, and marks are not overridable because each field has more than one entry.

To allocate memory for structure, use the structure name as the directive db, dw, etc. For example:

```
tom   birthday   ⟨1,5,50⟩
```

To refer to a field of a structure, use the structure name and the field name with a period. For example:

```
mov   al,tom.month         ;tom's month of birth → al
```

```
;
;              to define a structure for date of birth and names
;
;              name of record type = date
;              name of structure type = info
;
date       record     month:4, day:5, year:7
info       struc                          ;name of structure info
           name       db   '0123456789'   ;first field
                      db   0              ;2nd field
           birthday   dw   0              ;3rd field
info       ends                           ;end of structure defn
;
;              declare structure with name family as type info
;              it has 3 entries, each of the entry with only 1st field
;              defined and the 2nd and 3rd fields are filled with null
;
family     info       ⟨'dad'⟩             ;1st entry
           info       ⟨'mum'⟩             ;2nd entry
           info       ⟨'child'⟩           ;3rd entry
;
```

```
;
;                      store month of birth for each person
;
              mov    cx,3                    ;count = 3
              mov    bx,offset family        ;pointer to 1st entry
;
l__start:     push   cx                      ;save cx on stack
              mov    dx,offset msg__month    ;addr of mess to o/p → dx
              call   pstg                    ;output message
              lea    dx,[bx].name            ;load address of
                                             ;entry.name ('dad')
              call   pstg                    ;output name
              call   gnum                    ;read in ax
;
;                      store this in record field in birthday.month
;
              mov    dx,[bx].birthday        ;dx = birthday
              and    dx,not mask month       ;clear month.field
              mov    cl,month                ;shift count
              shl    ax,cl                   ;shift number to field
              or     dx,ax                   ;record → dx
              mov    [bx].birthday,dx        ;store updated birthday
;
;                      do the same with day and year
              ............
;
;                      update bx pointer points to next structure
;
              add    bx,size info            ;increase by size of info
              pop    cx                      ;retrieve count
              loop   l__start                ;dec cx and cont till cx=0
;
;                      to check birthdays using structures
;
l__2:         mov    dx,offset msg__month1   ;addr of o/p mess − 3 dx
              call   pstg                    ;o/p message
              call   gnum                    ;await an entry at the keyboard
              cmp    ax,0                     ;is entry = 0
              jz     l__2                     ;if yes, re-enter again
;
              mov    cx,3                     ;3 → cx
              mov    bx,offset family         ;addr of home → bx
;
;                      extract the month__field from the structure birthday
```

```
;
l__in2:    push   cx                    ;save cx on stack
           mov    dx,[bx].birthday      ;birthday__field → dx
           and    dx,mask month         ;extract the month field → dx
           mov    cl,month              ;bits to be shifted → cl
           shr    dx,cl                 ;right justify the month__field
           cmp    dx,ax                 ;cmp dx and ax
           jne    l__22                 ;jump to l__22
;
;          do the same for day
;
;
;                ......................................
;
           lea    dx,[bx].name          ;addr of o/p string → dx
           call   pstg                  ;o/p the string
           mov    dx,offset ms1         ;addr of o/p string → dx
           call   pstg                  ;o/p the string
;
;          update pointer for next structure
;
l__22      add    bx,size info          ;bx → bx + size of info
           pop    cx                    ;restore cx from stack
           loop   l__in2                ;dec cx & cont till cx = 0
           jmp    l__begin              ;jump to l__begin
;
;          message definition area
;
msg__month    db    'Enter month of birth of ',0
msg__month1   db    'Enter the month',0
ms1           db    ',  its your birthday  ',0ah,0dh,0
```

```
;
;          define a structure with the following elements
;
;
;          Student name           4 char
;          Student number         1 integer
;          Marks for English      1 integer
;                    Maths        1 integer
;                    History      1 integer
;                    Gen. Sci     1 integer
;
;
;          Initialize an array of structure with 4 elements.
;          Use this information to output the average marks of
;          each subject for all students.
;
```

```
          extrn   exit:far            ;return to op system
          extrn   pnum:far            ;output a number
          extrn   pline:far           ;output cf,lf
          extrn   putc:far            ;output character
          extrn   pstg:far            ;output string
;
code      segment
          assume  cs:code,ds:t__data,ss:stack
;
;         define structure sfile
;
sfile     struc
          sname         db    '0123'  ;Student name
                        db    0
          snum          dw    0        ;Student number
          eng__mark     dw    0        ;English mark
          math__mark    dw    0        ;Maths mark
          his__mark     dw    0        ;History mark
          sci__mark     dw    0        ;Gen Science mark
sfile     ends
;
;         initialization
;
go:       mov     ax,t__data
          mov     ds,ax               ;set ds
          mov     ax,stack
          mov     ss,ax               ;set ss
          mov     sp,offset top       ;set sp
;
;         output heading
;
          mov     dx,offset table
          call    pstg
          call    pline
;
;         main loop
;
          mov     cx,4                ;loop count
          mov     bx,offset student   ;base address
lp:       mov     ax,[bx].snum        ;structure element snum
          call    pnum                ;output student number
          mov     al,tabs
          call    putc
;
          lea     dx,[bx].sname
```

```
        call    pstg                    ;O/P student name
        mov     al,tabs
        call    putc
;
        mov     ax,[bx].eng__mark       ;get eng__mark
        add     sum[0],ax               ;Sum eng__mark
        call    pnum                    ;Print eng__mark
        mov     al,tabs
        call    putc
;
        mov     ax,[bx].math__mark      ;Get math__mark
        add     sum[2],ax               ;Sum math__mark
        call    pnum                    ;Print math__mark
        mov     al,tabs
        call    putc
;
        mov     ax,[bx].his__mark       ;Get his__mark
        add     sum[4],ax               ;Sum his__mark
        call    pnum                    ;Print his__mark
        mov     al,tabs
        call    putc
;
        mov     ax,[bx].sci__mark       ;Get SCI__mark
        add     sum[6],ax               ;Sum SCI__mark
        call    pnum                    ;Print SCI__mark
        call    pline
;
        add     bx,size student         ;Update bx to next record
        loop    lp                      ;repeat 3 times
;
;       print sums
;
        mov     dx,offset mess3         ;output label
        call    pstg
        mov     cx,4                    ;loop count
        mov     si,0                    ;index from 0
sum__lp: mov    ax,sum[si]
        call    pnum                    ;output sums
        mov     al,tabs
        call    putc
        inc     si
        inc     si                      ;next element
        loop    sum__lp                 ;repeat
        call    pline
;
```

```
;           print aves
;
;           mov     dx,offset mess4         ;o/p label
            call    pstg
            mov     cx,4                    ;loop count
            mov     si,0                    ;index from 0
;
ave__lp:    mov     ax,sum[si]
            cwd
            mov     bx,4
            div     bx                      ;ave=sum/4
            call    pnum
            mov     al,tabs
            call    putc
            inc     si
            inc     si                      ;next element
            loop    ave__lp                 ;repeat
;
            call    pline
            call    exit
code        ends
;
;           data area
;
t__data     segment
TABS        equ     9
table       db      'number   name   eng   maths   history   gen.   sci',0
;           initialize structure
mess3       db      TABS,'SUMS',TABS,0
mess4       db      TABS,'AVE.',TABS,0
student     sfile   ⟨'PETE',,1000,60,65,45,52⟩
            sfile   ⟨'JOHN',,1025,80,85,90,80⟩
            sfile   ⟨'DAVE',,1030,62,70,62,65⟩
            sfile   ⟨'STEV',,1045,73,12,68,70⟩
sum         dw      4 dup (0)
t__data     ends
;
stack       segment stack
            db      128 dup(?)
top         equ     $
stack       ends
            end     go
```

CHAPTER 13

Macros

The macro directives of the MACRO-86 assembler is a string replacement facility. Repeatedly-used sections of code are written once and then inserted at several places in the program. Together with the conditional assembly directives, sections of code can achieve compact configuration-dependent coding.

13.1 CONDITIONAL ASSEMBLY DIRECTIVES

Conditional assembly directives allow the user to design blocks of code which test for specific conditions and then proceed accordingly. Unwanted portions of code will be left unassembled.

All conditionals follow the format:

```
ifxxxx [argument]
    :   [else
    : ]   ENDIF
```

There are six conditional directives:

if ⟨exp⟩	;if ⟨exp⟩ evaluates to nonzero, the statements within the conditional block ;are assembled.
ife ⟨exp⟩	;if ⟨exp⟩ evaluates to 0, the statements ;in the conditional block are assembled.
if1	;Pass 1 conditional ;if the assembler is in pass 1, the ;statements in the conditional block are ;assembled.
if2	;Pass 2 conditional ;if the assembler is in pass 2, the

137

```
                        ;statements in the conditional block are
                        ;assembled.
    ifdef ⟨symbol⟩      ;if the ⟨symbol⟩ is defined or has been
                        ;declared external, the statements in the
                        ;conditional block are assembled.
    ifndef ⟨symbol⟩     ;if the ⟨symbol⟩ is not defined or not
                        ;declared external, the statements in the
                        ;conditional block are assembled.
```

Each IFxxxx must have a matching endif to terminate the conditional. Each conditional block may include the optional ELSE diretive, which allows alternate code to be generated when the opposite condition exists. Only one ELSE is permitted for a given if.

Conditionals may be nested. Any argument to a conditional must be known on pass 1 to avoid phase errors and incorrect evaluation. The assembler evaluates the conditional statement to true (nonzero value), or false (which equals 0). For example:

1. The assembler will send the message to the terminal, if CPM is defined as nonzero:

```
    if      cpm
    %out    *CPM version*              ;output string
    endif
```

2. One printout message is sent on each pass of the assembly:

```
    if1
    %out    *Pass 1 started*
    endif
```

```
    if2
    %out    *Pass 2 started*
    endif*
```

3. To produce one source program that can be included in systems that either have an 8087 processor or use 8086 procedures:

```
    ifdef   in8087
    use 8087 instructions here
    else
    use 8086 procedures to simulate floating point arith.
    endif
```

13.2 MACRO DIRECTIVES

The macro directive allows you to write blocks of code which can be repeated without recoding.

All macro definitions begin with the MACRO directive and end with the ENDM directives.

⟨name⟩   macro [⟨dummy⟩,....]   ;define macro with ⟨name⟩

....

endm

To use a macro, enter a macro call statement;

⟨name⟩   [⟨parameter⟩,....]

A parameter replaces a ⟨dummy⟩ on a one-to-one basis. The number of parameters is limited only by the length of the line. It need not be the same as the number of dummies in the macro definition. If there are more parameters than dummies, the extras are ignored. If there are fewer, the extra dummies will be made null.

purge ⟨macro-name⟩[,....]

Purge deletes the definition of the macro(s) listed after it. However, it is not necessary to purge a macro before redefining it. For example, to swap the contents of two variables:

Defining macro SWAP,

```
SWAP     macro arg1,arg2      ;;beginning of macro
         mov   ax,arg1        ;;arg 1 → ax
         xchg  arg2,ax        ;;exchange contents
         mov   arg1,ax        ;;ax → arg1
         endm                 ;;end of macro definition
```

To use the macro SWAP,

```
SWAP data1,data 2
```

generates the following instructions in the program

```
+   mov   ax,data1
+   xchg  data2,ax
+   mov   data1,ax
```

Special Macro Operators

Several special operators can be used in a macro block to select additional assembly functions:

1.   &   – to concatenate text
2.   ⟨text⟩ – to treat the text between the angle brackets as a single parameter
3.   ;;   – comment
4.   !   – to indicate that the next character is to be taken literally
5.   %   – to convert the expression that follows it to a number in the current radix.

Ampersand (&)

Ampersand concatenates text or symbols. A dummy parameter in a quoted string will not be substituted in an expansion unless preceded immediately by &. For example to output an ASCII char:

```
OUTCH       macro       arg1
            mov         al,'&arg1'      ;load al with char
            call        putc            ;call system fn
            endm
;
;     this procedure is called by
;
OUTCH       a                           ;call macro outch
```

generates

```
+   mov  al,'a'
+   call putc
```

Angle Brackets ⟨text⟩

Angle brackets cause MACRO-86 to treat the text between the angle brackets as a single literal. That is, all text within the angle brackets is seen as a single parameter, even if commas are used, and characters that have special functions (like;) are taken as literal characters. For example, to output a space using outch:

```
OUTCH⟨ ⟩    ;specify arg1 as a space character
```

Double Semicolons (;;)

A comment preceded by the two semicolons (;;) inside a macro is not saved as part of the expansion.

Exclamation (!)

An exclamation mark may be entered in an argument to indicate that the next character is to be taken literally. Therefore, !; is equivalent to ⟨;⟩.

Percent sign (%)

The percent sign is used only in a macro argument to convert the expression that follows to a number in the current radix. For example:

```
CR   is defined as a symbol
CR   equ   12
OUTNUM   %CR
```

generates

```
+   mov   ax,12
+   call pnum
```

LOCAL

```
local   ⟨dummy⟩[,⟨dummy⟩....]
```

The local directive is allowed only inside a macro definition block. A local statement must precede all other types of statement, including a comment (;) in the macro definition.

When local is executed, the assembler creates a unique symbol for each ⟨dummy⟩ and substitutes that symbol for each occurrence of the ⟨dummy⟩ in the expansion. These unique symbols are usually used to define a label within a macro, thus eliminating multiple-defined labels on successive expansions of the macro. For example:

1. To define a local label:

```
;
;       a macro that elements of destination array equals 5 added
;       to elements of source array both with length of len
;
ARRAYP5     macro   src,des,len     ;;beginning of macro
            local   lp__next        ;;local label used
            mov     cx,len          ;;array size → cx
            mov     si,0            ;;0 → index
lp__next:   mov     ax,src[si]      ;;load src array element
            add     ax,5            ;;ax = ax + 5
            mov     des[si],ax      ;;result = des array
            inc     si              ;;increment index

            loop    lp__next        ;;cont till count in cx=0
            endm                    ;;end of macro definition
```

To execute the macro,

        ARRAYP5 ary1,ary2,%count

count	equ	10	;length of array
ary1	db	10 dup (?)	;reserve 10 bytes for ary1
ary2	db	10 dup (0)	;reserve 10 bytes for ary2

generates

```
+              mov      cx,10
+              mov      si,0
+  ??0000:     mov      ax,ary1[si]
+              add      ax,5
+              mov      ary2[si],ax
+              inc      si
+              loop     ??0000
```

2. To define a local variable:

It is possible to use a locally defined variable in a macro only if the data segment and the code segment are declared as the same in the program:

```
;
;         display the message passed as the argument
;
OUTSTG    macrro  stg                     ;;beginning of macro outstg
          local   message,l__out          ;;local labels used
          jmp     l__out                  ;;jump to l__out
message   db      '&stg',0ah,0dh,0         ;;data with 1st arg and cr,lf
l__out:   mov     dx,offset message       ;;ds and cs must be the same
          call    pstg                    ;;display the message
          endm                            ;;end of this macro
     OUTSTG     (this is an error line)
```

generates

```
+              jmp      ??0002
+  ??00001     db       'this is an error line',0ah,0dh,0
+  ??0002      mov      dx,offset ??0001
+              call     pstg
```

If the data and code segment are declared as two different segments code and t__data, then the macro can read s:

```
;
;               display the message passed as the argument
;
OUTSTG    macro     stg               ;;beginning of macro outstg
          local     message           ;;local labels used
t__data   segment   public            ;;assume name of data segment in
                                       ;;main program is t__data
message   db '&stg',  0ah,0dh,0        ;;data with 1st arg and cr,lf
t__data   ends
          mov       dx,offset message
          call      pstg              ;;display the message
          endm                        ;;end of macro defn
```

3. Nested macros

```
;
;         a macro is referenced within another
;
OUTNUM    macro     arg1              ;;beginning of macro outnum
          mov       al,arg1           ;;entry arg1 → al
          cbw                         ;;al →ax
          call      pnum              ;;o/p number at the screen
          endm                        ;;end of this macro definition
OUTCH     macro     arg1              ;;beginning of macro outch
          mov       al,arg1           ;;entry arg1 → al
          call      putc              ;;o/p the char in al
          endm                        ;;end of this macro definition
OUTS      macro     fn,mem,len        ;;beginning of macro outs
          local     l__nx             ;;local label used
          mov       cx,len            ;;3rd arg → cx
          mov       bx,offset mem     ;;address of 2nd arg → bx
;
l__nx:    fn        [bx]              ;;reference 1st arg as macro
          inc       bx                ;;increment bx
          loop      l__nx             ;;dec cx & loop till cx = 0
          endm                        ;;end of this macro definition
```

To execute,

```
        OUTS   OUTNUM,ary1,10
```

The three arguments in outs are

```
fn   – outnum
mem – ary1
len  – 10
```

which expands into

```
mov     cx,10
mov     bx,offset ary1
??0002: OUTNUM      [bx]
        inc         bx
        loop        ??0002
```

It contains

```
OUTNUM    [bx]
```

which is a macro. Outnum expands into

```
mov   al,[bx]
cbw
call  pnum
```

Therefore the final expanded instructions are

```
+                    mov     cx,10
+                    mov     bx,offset ary1
+       ??0002:      OUTNUM  [bx]
+                    mov     al,[bx]
+                    cbw
+                    call    pnum
+                    inc     bx
+                    loop    ??0002
;
;   To call the macro again with fn = outch,
;
                     OUTS    OUTCH,ary2,10
+                    mov     cx,10
+                    mov     bx,offset ary2
+       ??0005:      OUTCH   [bx]
+                    mov     al,[bx]
+                    call    putc
+                    inc     bx
+                    loop    ??0005
```

Note that a different label ??0005 is generated to replace l__nx.

```
;
;       Use of macros
;       Define a macro to call the procedure written in Chapter 10
;       to display character strings on screen.
;
            extrn       exit:far                    ;exit to msdos
            extrn       clr:far                     ;clear screen
            extrn       gnum:far                    ;input an integer
            extrn       getc:far                    ;input a char
            extrn       pstg:far                    ;output a char string
            extrn       position:far                ;output string
;
;       define macro MSTG
;
MSTG        macro       col,line,attr,string
            local       m__mess,lp
            jmp         short lp
m__mess     db          '&string',0
lp:         mov         ax,'&attr'
            push        ax
            push        ds
            mov         ax,offset m__mess
            push        ax
            mov         ax,line
            push        ax
            mov         ax,col
            push        ax
            call        position
            endm
;
code        segment
            assume cs:code,ds:code,ss:stack
;
;           init segment registers
;
go:         mov         ax,code
            mov         ds,ax                       ;data segment
            mov         ax,stack
            mov         ss,ax                       ;init ss to stack
            mov         sp,offset s__data           ;set stack pointer
;
;           clear screen
;
            call        clr                         ;clear screen
;
```

```
                MSTG     10,10,⟨U⟩,⟨A C T⟩
                MSTG     60,15,⟨I⟩,⟨C T E C⟩
;
;               return to msdos
;
                call     exit
;
code            ends
;
stack           segment  stack
                db       128 deup(?)
s__data         equ      $
stack           ends
;
                end      go
```

CHAPTER 14

MSDOS Operating System Interface

This chapter presents the interface conventions which allow transient programs to access to MSDOS.

14.1 MSDOS

MSDOS is the most widely used disk operating system for personal computers based on Intel's 8086 and 8088 microprocessor.

It was initially designed by Seattle Computer Products in the US. In mid-1981, Microsoft Inc. bought all rights to the dos. IBM Shortly afterwards announced a personal computer with PC DOS, which is essentially the same as MSDOS. Microsoft has been continuously improving the DOS, supplying version 1.24 to IBM and the MSDOS version 1.25 as general release to all MSDOS users in March 1982. The new 2.0 version was released in February 1983, and is a substantial upgrade of the previous releases. Only the functions of the 1.25 version will be described here.

MSDOS enables the user to create and keep track of files, run and generate programs, and access peripheral devices, such as printers and disk drives, that are attached to the system. MSDOS can be used with many high-level languages, such as BASIC, Lang C, COBOL, and PASCAL. Most software packages like WORDSTAR, dBASE II, and Supercalc (which runs under CP/M 80) have been upgraded to run under MSDOS.

MSDOS reserves interrupt types 20 to 3f hex for its use. This means absolute locations 80h to 0ffh are the transfer address storage locations reserved by the operating system.

Function Requests

The user requests a function by placing a function number in the ah register, supplying additional information in other registers as necessary for the specific function, then executing an interrupt type 21h:

int   21h

When MS-DOS takes control it switches to an internal stack. User registers except ax are preserved unless information is passed back to the register as indicated in the specific requests.

These functions are divided into two main areas:

1. Device I/O
2. File access

14.2 SIMPLE DEVICE INPUT/OUTPUT

The functions are described in Table 14.1.

Table 14.1

Function no.	Description
1	Keyboard input
2	Video output
3	Auxiliary input
4	Auxiliary output
5	Printer output
6	Direct I/O
7	Direct console input
8	Console input without echo
9	Print string
10	Buffered keyboard input
11	Check keyboard status
12	Character input with buffer flush

Function 1:   Keyboard Input

Entry parameters:
register ah: 1

Return value:
register al: ASCII character

Waits for a character to be typed at the keyboard, then echoes the character to the video device and returns it in al. The character is checked for a ⟨ctrl C⟩. If this key is detected, an interrupt 23h, i.e. exit to msdos, will be executed.

Function 2:   Video Output

Entry parameters:
    register ah: 2
    register dl: ASCII character

Return value: None

The character in dl is output to the video device. If a ⟨ctrl C⟩ is detected after the output, an int 23h will be executed.

Function 3:   Auxiliary Input

Entry parameters:
    register ah: 3

Return value:
    register al: ASCII character

Waits for a character from the auxiliary input device, such as a secondary serial port, then returns that character in al.

Function 4:   Auxiliary Output

Entry parameters:
    register ah: 4
    register dl: ASCII character

Return value: None

The character in dl is output to the auxiliary device, such as a secondary serial port.

Function 5:   Printer Output

Entry parameters:
    register ah: 5
    register dl: ASCII character

Return value: None

The character in dl is output to the printer.

Function 6: Direct Console I/O

Entry parameters:
        register ah: 6
        register dl: ASCII character (output) or
                          0ffh (input)

Return value:
        register al: 0 if no keyboard input character or ASCII character

If dl is 0ffh, then al returns with the keyboard input character if one is ready, otherwise 0 will be returned in al. If dl is not 0ffh, then dl is assumed to have a valid character which is output to the video device. No checks are made on either input or output character for ⟨ctrl C⟩.

Function 7: Direct Console Input

Entry parameters:
        register ah: 7

Return value:

        register al: ASCII character

Waits for a character to be typed at the keyboard, then returns the character in al. As with function 6, no checks are made on the character.

Function 8: Console Input without Echo

Entry parameters:
        register ah: 8

Return value:
        register AL: ASCII character

This function is identical to function 1, except that the key is not echoed.
In summary, functions 1,6,7, and 8 are all input functions that vary according to Table 14.2.

Table 14.2

Function	Check ctrl-C	Echo character	Wait for keyboard
1	yes	yes	yes
6	no	no	no
7	no	yes	yes
8	yes	no	yes

Function 9:   Print String

Entry parameters:
  register ah: 9
  resgister ds:dx   pointer to a character string in memory

Return value: None

Each character in the string will be output to the video device as with function 2 until a '$' character is reached.

Function 10:   Buffered Keyboard Input

Entry parameters:
  register ah: 10
  register ds:dx   pointer to an input buffer

Return value: ASCII string

The buffered keyboard input function reads a line of edited console input into a buffer address by ds:dx. Console input is terminated when a carriage return is typed. The read buffer takes the form:

ds:dx	+0	+1	+2	+3	+4	......	+n
	mx	nc	c1	c2	c3		??

where mx is the maximum number of characters which the buffer will hold (1 to 255), and must be initialized before calling the function. Location ds:dx+1 (nc) is set by the operating system upon return, and it is equal to the number of characters read, followed by the characters c1, c2,..., cn read from the console.

Function 11:   Check Keyboard Status

Entry parameters:
    register   ah: 11

Return value:
    register al: status

If a character is available from the keyboard, al will contain 0ffh in return; otherwise al will be 0.

Function 12: Character Input with Buffer Flush

Entry parameters:
    register ah: 12
    register al: 1,6,7,8,10

Return value:
    register al: ASCII character

First the keyboard type-ahead buffer is emptied. Then if al is 1,6,7,8, or 10, the corresponding MSDOS input function is executed If al is not one of these values, no further operation is carried out and al returns 0.

These functions are used in the procedures described in earlier chapters for standard input/output and are listed in Appendix B.

14.3 FILE ACCESS

File Control Block (FCB)

The file control block data area consists of a sequence of 33 bytes for sequential access and a series of 37 bytes in the case where the file is accessed randomly. Each file being accessed through the operating system must have a corresponding FCB which provides the name and allocation information for all subsequent file operations. The FCB format is defined as follows:

byte 0   Drive code
                = 0 default drive
                = 1 drive A
                = 2 drive B, etc.

byte 1–8   File name

If the file is less than 8 characters, the name must be left justified with trailing blanks.

byte 9–11   Extension to file name
             If less than 3 characters, must be left justified with trailing blanks

byte 12–13   Current block (extent)
             Specifies the current block number of 128 records, starting from 0

byte 14–15   Record size
             Default to 128; it may be changed after an open file operation

byte 16–19   File size
             Current size of the file in bytes

byte 20–21   Date
             bit 0–4, day of month;
             bit 5–8, month of year;
             bit 9–15, year from 1980

byte 22–23   Time
             bit 0–4, second/2;
             bit 5–10, minutes;
             bit 11–15, hours

byte 24–31   Reserved for MSDOS

byte 32   Current record number

byte 33–36   Random record number

Function 13:   Disk Reset

Entry parameters:
    register ah: 13

Return value: None

Flush all file buffers. Unclosed files that have been changed in size will not be properly recorded in the disk directory until they are closed. This function need not be called before a disk change if all files which have been written have been closed.

Function 14:   Select Disk

Entry parameters:
File input/output
register ah: 14
register dl: 0 = drive A
                     1 = drive B, etc.

Return value:
register al: total number of drives

The drive specified in dl is selected as the default disk.

Table 14.3

Function no.	Description
13	Disk reset
14	Select disk
25	Current disk
15	Open file
16	Close file
19	Delete file
22	Create file
23	Rename file
41	Parse file name
26	Set disk transfer address
20	Sequential read
21	Sequential write
33	Random read
34	Random write
36	Set random record field
39	Random block read
40	Random block write

Function 25:   Current Disk

Entry parameters:
register ah: 25

Return value:
register al: current default disk
                    0, drive A

1, drive B, etc.

al returns the code of the current default drive.

Function 15:   Open File

Entry parameters:
    register ah: 15
    register ds:dx   Unopened file control block

Return value:
    register al: 0 if successful
                         0ffh if the named file is not found

The open file operation is used to activate a file which currently exists in the disk directory.

Function 16:   Close File

Entry parameters:
    register ah: 16
    register ds:dx   an opened file control block

Return value:
    register al: 0 if successful
                         0ffh of the named file is not found

This function must be called after the file has been updated to ensure that all directory information is updated.

Function 19:   Delete File

Entry parameters:
    register ah: 19
    register ds:dx   Unopened FCB

Return value:
    register al: 0 successful
                         0ffh if file not found

All matching directory entries are deleted.

Function 22:   Create File

Entry parameters:
    register ah: 22
    register ds:dx   Unopened FCB

Return value:
    register al: 0 successful

Offh if disk directory is full

The disk directory is searched for an empty entry, the entry is initialized to a zero-length file, and the file is opened (see function 15).

Function 23:   Rename File

Entry parameters:

register ah:	23
register ds:dx	Modified FCB

Return value:

register al:	= 0 successful
	= 0ffh if no match was found

The modified FCB has a drive code and file name, and a second file name starting at ds:dx+11h. If '?'s appear in the second name, then the corresponding positions in the original name will be unchanged.

Function 41   Parse File name

Entry parameters:

register ah:	41
register ds:si	Command line to parse
es:di	Unopened FCB
al	Bit 0 = 1, at most one leading file name separator will be ignored
	i.e. all parsing stops if a separator is encountered.
al	Bit 1–3, determine what to do if the drive, filename, or extension, respectively, are missing.

Return value:

register al:	00 if successful
	01 if either '?' or '*' appears in the filename

To parese the filename in the command line, if al bits 1–3 are zero, and the field is not present, then the FCB is filled with a fixed value (0, meaning the default drive for the drive field; all blanks for the filename and extension fields). If the bit is a 1, and the field is not present on the command line, then that field in the destination FCB at es:di is left unchanged.

Function 26:   Set Disk Transfer Address

Entry parameters:

register ah:	26
register ds:dx	Disk transfer address

Return value: None

The disk transfer address is set to ds:dx. MSDOS will not allow disk transfers to wrap around within the segment, nor to overflow into the next segment.

Function 20: Sequential Read

Entry parameters:
    register ah: 20
    register ds:dx   Opened FCB

Return value:
    register al: 00 if successful
                    01 if no data in record
                    02 if not enough mem for transfer
                    03 if a partial record is read

The record addressed by the current block and current record is loaded at the disk transfer address, then the record address is incremented.

Function 21: Sequential Write

Entry parameters:
    register ah: 21
    register ds:dx   Opened FCB

Return value:
    register al: 00 if successful
                    01 if disk full
                    02 if not enough mem for transfer

The record addressed by the current block and current record fields is written from the disk transfer address, then the record address is incremented.

```
;
;        DUMP.ASM MSDOS UTILITY FOR 8086
;
;
;        Procedures defined in stdio
;
         extrn  putc:far          ;output a char
         extrn  pnumh:far         ;output in hex
         extrn  pline:far         ;output newline
         extrn  pstg:far          ;output string
         extrn  pascii:far        ;output ascii or '.'
         extrn  exit:far          ;proc to return to msdos
;
code     segment                  ;beginning of segment code
         assume cs:code,ds:code,ss:stack; various segments used
;
;        define symbols
;
DOS      equ    21h               ;msdos function entry point
OPENFL   equ    0fh               ;msdos id for opening file
```

```
SETDMA equ      1ah                     ;msdos id for set dma
READFL equ      14h                     ;msdos id for read file
PARSEFLequ      29h                     ;msdos id for parse filename
;
;               define structure
;
fcb       struc                         ;fcbstruc definition
drive     db    0                       ;the drive used
filename  db    '                       ;the filename
ftype     db    '   '                   ;the file type
fext      dw    0                       ;file extent
frecord   dw    128                     ;file record size
fsize     dd    0                       ;file size
fdate     dw    0                       ;creation date
ftime     dw    0                       ;creation time
fresv     db    8 dup (?)               ;file reserve block size
fcr       db    0
frand     dd    0

fcb       ends                          ;end of structure definition
;
;               macro definitions
;
OUTNUM          macro   arg1            ;beginning of this macro outnum
                mov     ah,ARG1         ;calling parameter → ah
                mov     al,arg1[1]      ;content addressed by arg1 → al
                call    pnumh           ;o/p content of al in hex
                endm                    ;end of this macro definition
;
OUTCH           macro   arg1            ;beginning of this macro outch
                mov     al,arg1         ;calling parameter → al
                call    putc            ;o/p content of al
                endm                    ;end of this macro definition
;
OUTSTG          macro   stg             ;beginning of macro definition
                local   message,l__out  ;local labels used
                jmp     l__out          ;jump to l__out
message         db      '&stg',0ah,0dhg,0 ;data definitions
l__out:         mov     dx,offset message ;address string to be o/p → dx
                call    pstg            ;o/p the string
                endm                    ;end of this macro definition
;
;
;
;               main module begin from loc go
;
;               init segment registers
```

```
;
go:        mov     ax,code
           mov     ds,ax               ;init ds to code
           mov     ax,stack
           mov     ss,ax               ;init ss to stack
           mov     sp,offset s__data   ;set stack pointer
;
;          output signon message

           OUTSTG ⟨BCY Copyright (C) 1983⟩
;
;          parse file name
;
           les     di,fcbptr           ;pointer to fcb
           lds     si,comptr           ;pointer to command line
           mov     ah,PARSEFL          ;msdos fn
           mov     al,0                ;stop after 1 file separator
           int     DOS                 ;msdos function entry point
;
;          reset ds
;
           mov     ax,code
           mov     ds,ax               ;reset ds to code
;
;          open file
;
l__op6:    mov     ah,OPENFL           ;msdos id for opening file
           mov     dx,offset sfcb      ;sfcb address → dx
           int     DOS                 ;msdos function entry point
           inc     al                  ;increment al to detect error
           jnz     l__ok               ;jump if not 0, means no error
;
;          file open error
;
           OUTSTG ⟨file does not exit⟩  ;o/p specified string
           call    exit                ;return to msdos
;
;          set DMA address
;
l__ok:     mov     ah,SETDMA           ;msdos id for set dma → ah
           mov     dx,offset sbuf      ;dma address → dx
           int     DOS                 ;msdos function entry point
;
;          beginning of main loop
;          read a sector
;
```

```
l__main:   mov     ah,READFL              ;msdos id for read file → ah
           mov     dx,offset sfcb         ;fcb address
           int     DOS                    ;msdos function entry point
;
;          check if read error
;
           cmp     al,1                   ;check if al = 1, means EOF
           jz      l__eof                 ;jump if yes
;
;          set length of each block during output
;
           mov     cx,8                   ;length = 8 → cx
           mov     bx,offset sbuf         ;beginning of buffer → bx
;
;          o/p location of the byte to be dumped
;
l__loc:    push    cx                     ;save length, cx on stack
           push    bx                     ;save buffer address on stack
           mov     ax,loc                 ;content of loc → ax
           call    pnumh                  ;o/p content of ax in hex
;
;          o/p two spaces
;
           OUTCH   ⟨' '⟩                  ;output a space
           OUTCH   ⟨' '⟩                  ;output a space
           mov     cx,2                   ;set no of blocks → cx = 2
;
;          o/p data in hex
;
l__hex0:   push    cx                     ;save block count → cx
;
;          set number of words in a block
;
           mov     cx,4                   ;no of words in a block → cx=4
l__hex:    OUTNUM⟨[bx]⟩                   ;o/p the char addressed by bx
;
;          separate each word by a space
;
           OUTCH   ⟨' '⟩                  ;o/p a space
           inc     bx                     ;increment buffer ptr
           inc     bx                     ;  twice
           loop    short l__hex           ;jump to l__hex till cx = 0
;
;          separate two horz blocks by two spaces
;
           OUTCH   ⟨' '⟩                  ;o/p a space
```

```
                OUTCH    〈'   '〉              ;o/p a space
;
;          next horz block
;
                pop      cx                    ;restore no of block → cx
                loop     l__hex0               ;loop till cx = 0
;
;          output data in ascii
;
                pop      bx                    ;restore buffer point → bx
                mov      cx,16                 ;no of chars in a line → 16
l__asc:         mov      al,[bx]               ;char addressed by bx → al
                call     pascii                ;o/p char in al in ascii
                inc      bx                    ;increment buffer pointer
                loop     short l__asc          ;cont till cx = 0
                call     pline                 ;o/p a CR LF
;
;          updates counters for next line
;
                add      loc,16                ;loc = loc + 16
                pop      cx                    ;restore total no of block → cx .
                loop     l__loc                ;loop till cx = 0
;
                call     pline                 ;o/p a CR LF
                jmp      l__main               ;jump to main loop
;
;          end of file detected
;
l__eof:         call     exit                  ;return to msdos
;
loc             dw       0                     ;location in the printing record
sbuf            db       128 dup(?)            ;128 byte for record read
sfcb            fcb      〈,'    '''〉            ;fcb
comptr          dd       02d00002h             ;command line pointer
fcbptr          dd       sfcb                  ;fcb pointer
code            ends                           ;end of this code segment
;
;
;          stack segments
;
stack           segment  stack                 ;beginning of stack segment
                db       128 dup(?)            ;reserve 256 bytes for stack
s__data         equ      $                     ;top of stack is s__data
stack           ends                           ;end of this stack segment
                end      go                    ;end of program
;
```

```
;                      print.asm ms-dos utility for 8086
;

                extrn       pstg:far
                extrn       putc:far
                extrn       pline:far
                extrn       clr:far
                extrn       exit:far
                extrn       getc:far
;
code            segment
                assume cs:code, ds:code, ss:stack
;
;               set system equates
;
DOS             equ         21h
OPENF           equ         0fh
SETDMA          equ         1ah
READF           equ         14h
PARSEF          equ         29h
CR              equ         0dh
;
;               define fcb structure
;
fcb             struc
drive           db          0
filename        db          '      '
ftype           db          '   '
fext            dw          0
frec            dw          128
fsize           dd          0
fdate           dw          0
ftime           dw          0
fres            db          8 dup (?)
fcr             db          0
frand           db          0
fcb             ends
;
go:             mov         ax,code              ;initialize seg reg.
                mov         ds,ax
                mov         ax,stack
                mov         ss,ax
                mov         sp,offset top
;
;               parse filename from command line
;
                les         di,fcbptr            ;set param
```

```
          lds     si,comptr            ;set param
          mov     ah,PARSEF            ;accept filename
          mov     al,0                 ;1 arg in command line
          int     DOS                  ;system call
;
;         reset data segment
;
          mov     ax,code
          mov     ds,ax                ;code → ds
;
;         open file
;
          mov     ah,OPENF             ;set open
          mov     dx,offset sfcb       ;address fcb
          int     DOS                  ;system call
          inc     al                   ;test file opened
          jnz     begin
;
;         open error
;
          mov     dx,offset mess
          call    pstg
          call    exit                 ;terminate
;
;         set dma address
;
begin:    mov     ah,SETDMA
          mov     dx,offset buffer     ;read location
          int     DOS                  ;system call
;
;         main program
;
          call    clr                  ;clear screen
          mov     cx,22                ;set count 22 lines
;
;         read 128 byte block of data
;
read_lp:  mov     bx,offset buffer
          mov     ah,READF             ;set read function
          mov     dx,offset sfcb
          int     DOS                  ;system call
          cmp     al,1                 ;check eof
          jz      eof
;
main:     mov     al,[bx]              ;get next char
          call    putc                 ;output char
```

```
                cmp     al,CR                       ;check carriage return
                jnz     next__char
;
;               end of line, test screen end
;
                dec     cx
                jnz     next__char
;
;               prompt for response
;
                call    pline
                push    dx
                mov     dx,offset mess1             ;prompt next screen
                call    pstg
                call    getc                        ;wait for a character
                mov     cx,22                       ;reset line count
                call    clr                         ;clear screen
                call    pline                       ;new line
                pop     dx
;
next__char      label   near
                inc     bx                          ;plus 1 character pointer
                cmp     bx,offset buffer+128
                jz      read__lp
                jmp     main                        ;next character
;
;               end of file
;
eof:            call    pline
                call    exit                        ;exit
;
;               data area
;
buffer          db      128 dup(?)                  ;dma buffer
sfcb            fcb     ⟨,'      ',      '⟩         ;file control block
comptr          dd      02c00102h                   ;command line ptr
fcbptr          dd      sfcb                        ;fcb ptr
mess            db      'open error',0
mess1           db      'type ⟨cr⟩ to continue ',0
code            ends
;
stack           segment stack
                db      128 dup(?)
top             equ     $
stack           ends
                end go
```

CHAPTER 15

Interfacing with BASIC

Application programs that are written in a high-level language like BASIC suffer the disadvantages of speed and limited utilities, such as the direct operating system interfacing described in the previous chapter. Provisions are made for BASIC programs to execute user-written assembly language subroutines. Section 15.1 suggests methods of loading the assembly routines. The BASIC CALL statement is used to interface the 8086 assembly language with BASIC-86, with the rules of parameter-passing via this statement being defined in Section 15.2.

15.1 MEMORY ALLOCATION

In executing a MS-BASIC program which calls an assembly language routine, memory space must be set aside for each routine before it can be loaded. During initialization, the M: switch can be used. For example:

MSBASIC   /M:32768   ;use first 32K of memory for BASIC

MSBASIC   /M:H0F000   ;use first 56K of memory for BASIC

The assembly language subroutines are defined as procedures with the type far. They must not contain any other far references.

After they are assembled, they can be loaded in a BASIC program using the POKE statement, or the BLOAD statement. Using compiled BASIC, both assembly language and basic modules can be linked together to produce the executable file.

POKE statement

The BASIC POKE I,J statement moves a byte into a memory location. The integer expression I is the offset address of the memory location after the last DEF SEG statement, and J is the data.

A simple assembly procedure is loaded into memory in the following BASIC program, to display the character A on the screen:

```
1000  DEF SEG=&HF00        'define segment base address
1010  PTR=0                'define memory offset from base
1020  NSIZE=19             'number of bytes to load
1030  FOR L%=1 TO NSIZE    'begin of loop
1040  READ A%              'get binary code
1050  POKE PTR%,A%         'move to memory specified by ptr%
1060  PTR% = PTR% + 1      'update to next byte
1070  NEXT                 'repeat for all data
1071  PRINT CHR$(27) + "E" 'clear screen
1072  PRO% = 0             'subroutine address
1074  CALL PRO%            'execute assembly lang. routine
1076  SYSTEM               'return to system
1080  DATA &H06,&H1E,&H0B8,&H0,&H0F0      ' all data
1090  DATA &H8E,&H0C0,&H0B4,&H00
1100  DATA &H0B0,&H0A5,&H26,&H0A3,0,0
1200  DATA & H1F,&H07,&H0CB
1220  DATA  0
```

When there are a large number of assembly subroutines, entering all the binary code as data in a BASIC program is very time-consuming, and may lead to errors. The BASIC BLOAD and BSAVE statement should be used instead.

BLOAD

The BLOAD statement in BASIC allows direct disk access to files in binary format:

>   BLOAD 'filename' memory address

where filename is a legal filename, and memory address is the memory address.

Unfortunately the BLOAD statement will not directly load in files which are not created using the BASIC BSAVE statement.

BSAVE

The BSAVE statement in BASIC copies the content of specified memory locations to disk:

>   BSAVE 'filename' memory address, size

where filename is a legal filename, memory address is the start address for save, and size is the total number of bytes.

The process required to create a file containing the assembly routines for BASIC to be loaded into memory at run time is as follows:

1. Create executable file from assembly modules
2. Load in high memory
3. Run MS-BASIC to save the memory contents.

The whole process could be carried out in DEBUG. For example, let an assembly routine be created and assembled and linked to create an executable file (say BASASM.EXE). Because there will not be a stack segment, a warning message,

   no stack segment

will be produced by the MS-linker.
   Use DEBUG to allocate the segment address used by BASIC:

DEBUG MSBASIC.COM

R ⟨cr⟩
   ... CS=CCCC, DS=DDDD, SS=SSSS, ES=EEEE, IP=XXXX

Q ⟨cr⟩

Note the values of CCCC, DDDD, SSSS, EEEE, and XXXX. In most systems, the values of CCCC, DDDD, SSSS, and EEEE are all equal to 473, and XXXX is 0100h.
   Use DEBUG to load the BASASM.EXE file into memory, and relocate it at high memory:

DEBUG BASASM.EXE

allocates the binary object code as CS:100, examines this value, and moves it to a high memory address (say 0f00:0):

   M start-address,size,destination address

Change all the segment registers to those given above: CCCC, DDDD, etc.

   RCS ⟨cr⟩
      CCCC ⟨cr⟩   ;replace by the CCCC value as above
   RSS ⟨cr⟩
     SSSS ⟨cr⟩
   RIP ⟨cr⟩
      XXXX

.. etc. .

and load in MS-BASIC

```
N  MSBASIC.COM ⟨cr⟩
L  ⟨cr⟩
G  ⟨cr⟩
```

Now execute the following statements:

```
1000 DEF SEG = &H0F00 'SET SEGMENT ADDRESS TO HIGH MEMORY
1010 BSAVE "BASASM.BLD",0,128 'SAVE WITH NO. OF BYTE
1020 SYSTEM
RUN
```

This should make a copy of the content of memory address of 0f000h on disk, then return to DEBUG.

Quit the debugger, and reload MS-BASIC:

```
MSBASIC   /M:HF000
```

Then to load the procedure at run time:

```
1000  DEF SEG = &H0F00
1010  BLOAD "BASASM.BLD",0
```

BASCOM

The MS-BASIC compiler BASCOM generates object modules from a BASIC program coded and written to disk with the BASIC interpreter (i.e. 'saved' with the 'A' option). Object modules produced by MACRO-86 and BASCOM are linked using MS-LINK. The resultant executable file (–.EXE) may then be run simply by typing the name given to it during the link. Each assembly language module name must be defined as public for the linker to satisfy all external labels.

15.2 USING THE CALL STATEMENT

After the binary codes are loaded into memory using one of the methods described in the above section, the BASIC CALL statement is recommended to interface 8086 assembly language routines with MS-BASIC:

CALL ⟨variable name⟩ [⟨argument list⟩]

where variable name contains the address of the beginning of the procedure being executed, and argument list contains the variables or constants, separated by commas, that are passed to the routine.

Invoking the CALL statement causes the following to occur. MS-BASIC passes its parameters by address via the stack, i.e. the address of each parameter within the data segment is pushed onto the stack. When the argument is a string, the value that is passed onto the stack is an address to a 3-byte data called the 'string descriptor'. Byte 0 of the string descriptor contains the length of the string (0–255). Bytes 1 and 2 are the address of the string.

MS-BASIC executes an assembler call instruction with the label defined as far with cs given in the last DEF SEG statement, and the offset value given in ⟨variable name⟩.

Registers ax, bx, cx, dx, si, di, and bp can all be used without saving their contents on stack.

The assembly routine must execute a ret n instruction to pop all the parameters off the stack. For example, the following assembly routine requires four parameters on entry for the column, row, attribute, and the text string for direct memory-mapped display:

```
;
code            segment
                assume cs:code
;
;               define procedure
;               display strings at col,row with attribute att
;
position        proc            far
;
;               on entry :-
;               sp+10           – string descriptor
;               sp+8            – character attribute
;               sp+6            – y co-ord on the screen
;               sp+4            – x co-ord on the screen
;               sp,sp+2         – return address
;
;               define arguments on stack
;
xc              equ   word ptr [bp+8]
yc              equ   word ptr [bp+10]
att             equ   word ptr [bp+12]
stg             equ   word ptr [bp+14]
;
;               save registers
;
                push   ds
                push   es
```

```
                mov       bp,sp
;
;               display characters
;
                mov       ax,0f000h          ;load base of screen address
                mov       es,ax              ;extre segment register = 0f000h
;
;               calculate start address on screen
;
;               base = y * 160 + x * 2
;
                mov       bx,yc              ;get address of yc
                mov       ax,[bx]            ;content of yc
                mov       cx,160
                imul      cx                 ;y * 160
                mov       dx,ax
                mov       bx,xc
                mov       ax,[bx]
                add       ax,ax              ;2 * x
                add       dx,ax              ;dx = base
;
;               output string
;
                mov       bx,att             ;address of att
                mov       ah,0
                mov       al,[bx]            ;content of att
                cmp       al,'I'             ;inverse
                jnz       l_0
                mov       ah,80h
                jmp       short  l_begin
l_0:            cmp       al,'H'             ;half intensity
                jnz       l_2
                mov       ah,40h
                jmp       short  l_begin
l_2:            cmp       al,'U'             ;underline
                jnz       l_begin
                mov       ah,20h
;
;               display chars
;
l_begin:        mov       bx,stg
                mov       cl,[bx]            ;size of string
                mov       ch,0
                jcxz      quit
                mov       si,[bx+1]          ;address
```

```
                mov     bx,dx
;
l__nxchar:      mov     al,ds:[si]      ;get string
                add     al,100          ;set font address
                mov     es:[bx],ax      ;display on screen
                inc     bx
                inc     bx              ;update to next screen pos.
                inc     si              ;next char on string
                loop    l__nxchar       ;repeat for all string char
;
;               retrieve segment registers
;
quit:           mov     sp,bp
                pop     ds
                pop     es
                ret     8
position        endp
code            ends
                end
```

After saving the assembly language routine on disk in BAS4.BLD say, to run
the program under MS-BASIC, the following BASIC statements can be used:

```
1000  DEF SEG = &HF00              'define segment base address
1010  BLOAD "BAS4.BLD",0           'load assembly lang. module
1012  PRINT CHR$(27)+"E"           'clear screen
1020  COL% = 10                    '10 → column
1030  ROW% = 5                     '5 → row
1040  ATT% = ASC ("U")             "U' → att
1045  STG$ = "ACT"                 "ACT' → stg
1050  PRO% = 0                     'assembly lang routine start addr.
1060  CALL PRO%(STG$,ATT%,ROW%,COL%)   'exec
1070  ATT% = ASC("I")              "U' → att
1080  COL% = 68                    '68 → column
1090  ROW% = 20                    '20 → row
2000  CALL PRO%(STG$,ATT%,ROW%,COL%)   'exec
2100  STOP                         ;end
```

CHAPTER 16

Intercomputer Communications

In the age of the electronic mail, communications systems are widely connected to the telephone network of the country. This enables letters, documents, and files to be sent from computer to computer nationwide. The ACT Micromail is a complete package for linking the ACT computer into such a network in Britain.

In this chapter, a simple method of connection of two Sirius computers to provide a facility for memory-to-memory file transfer is described.

16.1 SERIAL INTERFACE

The 'standard' which has been adopted for most serial interfaces between two micros is known as 'RS232'. It is a standard of the American Electronic Industries Association, specifying the electrical characteristics of the interface signals, along with the shape and pin assignments of the connectors to be used.

Each unit of data can be set to transmit or receive 5, 6, 7, or 8-bit characters, with 8-bit being the most commonly used. These characters are sent with the least significant bit first. Binary bits '1' and '0' are represented by voltages along the line.

When there is no data transfer, the communication line is low. To identify the beginning of a character, a 'start' bit which is high prefixes each character. One or two 'stop' bits which are always low are sent to suffix each character. Such an arrangement will enable the two devices to keep in step.

An error-checking method is to set the parity convention with a 'parity' bit. When the sender transmits a character, it counts the number of '1' bits in the character, and if the sum is even, it sets the 'parity' bit to '1'; otherwise a '0' bit is sent (the even parity mode).

Before communication can be established, both sender and receiver must be set to the same nominal communication speed. This speed is measured in bits-per-second (baud rate). Commonly used rates are 300 baud for modems communicating via telephone, or 4800 or 9600 baud via cable links.

Thus a representation of the letter 'A' (ASCII 41h) can be found as,

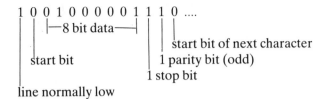

```
1 0 0 1 0 0 0 0 0 1 1 1 0 ....
    |—8 bit data—|    | | |
                      | | |start bit of next character
                      | |1 parity bit (odd)
  start bit           |1 stop bit
                      
line normally low
```

The Sirius 1 uses the NEC 7201 multiprotocol serial communications controller (MPSC2) to give two channels for data transfers. The controller is memory mapped and programmable.

When two Sirius 1 computers are connected together via a simple cable link as shown here, files can be transferred from one computer to another:

```
pin                             pin
 1  ———————————————————————      1   Ground
 2  ———————————————————————      3   Receive data
 3  ———————————————————————      2   Trans data
 7  ———————————————————————      7   Signal ground
 5  ─┐                    ┌─      5   Clear to send
 6  ─┤                    ├─      6   Data set ready
 8  ─┤                    ├─      8   Data carrier detect
20  ─┘                    └─     20   Data terminal ready
```

16.2 TRANSMISSION SPEED

The ACT Sirius has a 8253 timer device to provide the clock input for both the serial ports. The baud rate can therefore be programmed to run between 300 and 19 200.

The control ports are set at memory address e0020 – e0023; that is:

20 – set baud rate for port a
21 – set baud rate for port b
23 – control register for the timer device

```
;
;            ACT sirus comms procs
;
;            set baud rate to 4800 for serial port
;
baud      proc      near
          mov       ax,0e002h          ;es = base port address
          mov       es,ax
```

;

```
        mov     byte ptr es:[3],54          ;set control register
        mov     byte ptr es:[PDATA],10h  ;baud rate low byte
        mov     byte ptr es:[PDATA],0    ;baud rate high byte
        ret
baud    endp
```

The values of PDATA are

	Port A	Port B
PDATA	0	1

The values (in radix 16) for the different baud rates are shown in Table 16.1.

Table 16.1

Baud rate	Low byte	High byte
300	0	1
600	80	0
1200	40	0
2400	10	0
4800	10	0
9600	8	0
19200	4	0

16.3 TRANSMIT/RECEIVE DATA

Before the system can be used for serial communications, it must be properly initialized.

Control Word (CWORD)

The default parameters for serial transfer on the ACT are, 8-bit data, 1 stop bit, and no parity bit. The control word is 8-bit, as defined in Table 16.2, starting from the most significant bit MSB.

CWORD = 01000111 for transmission with 1 stop bit and 1 parity bit in even parity mode.

The CWORD is part of the memory-mapped device at address 0e0024h–0e0043h. It is possible to change this configuration with a simple software operation.

Table 16.2

Bit	Description
MSB 0–1	Clock rate – specifies the relationship between the transmitter and the receiver clock inputs and the actual data rate. 00–1 ×data rate 01–16 × data rate 10–32 × data rate 11–64 × data rate For the clock rate used above, 01 must be used.
2–3	Sync mode – this field is ignored in asynchronous mode, set to 00.
4–5	Stop bit – specifies the number of bit times used as the stop bit length by the transmitter. The receiver always checks for one stop bit. 00 – sync mode 01 – 1 stop bit 10 – 1.5 stop bits 11 – 2 stop bits
6	Parity even/odd – specifies even or odd parity mode when enabled. 0 – odd parity 1 – even parity
7	Parity enable – setting this bit to 1 adds an extra data bit containing parity information to each transmitted character. Each received character is expected to contain this extra bit and the receiver parity checker is enabled.

```
mov     ax,0e004h                    ;port base address
mov     es,ax
mov     byte ptr es:[PSTAT],4        ;addressing control reg 4
mov     byte ptr es:[PSTAT],CWORD    ;control word
```

The values of PSTAT are

	Port A	Port B
PSTAT	2	3

Transmit Data

The SEND procedure is responsible for sending data in memory to the communication control via a MOV instruction:

```
;
send      proc     near
;
;         on entry
;         es –     0e004h   base address for comm port
;         al –     data
;
ls__noop: mov      dl,es:[PSTAT]        ;read status byte
          and      dl,04               ;read ready bit
          jz       ls__noop            ;repeat check if not ready
          mov      es:[PDATA],al       ;output char to port
          ret
send      endp
```

Receive Data

The RECEIVE procedure is used to accept a character from the controller:

```
;
;         receive
receive   proc near
;
;         receive read char from port
;
;         on entry :–
;
;         es 0e004 (base port address)
;         return :–
;         al = data
;
lr__rd:   mov      al,es:[PSTAT]
          and      al,01               ;read status
          jnz
          mov      lr__ok              ;data is ready
receive   endp     al,es:[PDATA]       ;read data → al
```

16.4 COMMUNICATION PROTOCOL

To ensure correct interpretation of a sequential stream of bytes, a communication protocol that imposes meaning on the data stream must be specified. Computer protocols are specified precisely for the two systems.

After the initialization of files in the transmit and receive program, an initial handshaking procedure is required to establish whether the link is active, i.e. an acknowledge (ACK) is sent to the receiver, and there is a delay until a negative acknowledge (NAK) is received. Some systems impose a time limit on this wait state, such that the program will terminate with an error message.

To encode meaning into a block of data (a frame), a beginning-of-frame marker, the data, and an end-of-frame marker must be included. A checksum can also be included in each frame to enable more reliable communications along a noisy link.

As one possible design, the structure of a data frame is described. Each frame has a fixed length. After the SOH is sent, the sector number and its complement are sent. While each item of data is sent, a check sum equal to the sum of all data in mod 8 is accumulated, and sent after each 128 bytes of data. The receive program then checks this with its own calculated checksum.

The program then either acknowledges with an ACK character, or the whole is re-transmitted when an error is detected. The process is repeated for a number of sectors (8 in the case of 86send and 86rec) before the disk read and write procedure is called.

An end-of-take (EOT) marker is sent when all data in the source file is transmitted:

SOH	Sector number	−sector number	128 data bytes	checksum

A complete listing of a transmit and receive program is given in Appendix C. The transmit program requires the filename for sending in the command line, for example:

86SEND MYFILE.TXT

and the receive program will create a file with the name specified in the command line, and save all the data from the communication port onto disk:

86REC MYFILE.TXT

CHAPTER 17

Audio Subsystem Programming

Speed synthesisers are not only found in video games, but also in sophisticated warning devices on production lines, telling people of critical errors. Serious research is also being carried out on behalf of disabled and handicapped people.

The ACT audio package provides a powerful addition to the system through packages utilizing the voice generator. The theory and its implementation is described in this chapter.

17.1 DIGITIZED SPEECH

Computers communicate in a digital language, while human language is analogue. A number of techniques have therefore been devised which allow a computer to synthesize a human voice.

Some synthesized voices employ electronic circuitry to simulate the throat and vocal tract, while others use digital recording.

The basic concepts of digital speech are fairly simple. A voice can be entered via the audio input. Through an analogue-to-digital (A/D) converter, each voice waveform can be stored as binary numbers. The number of samples varies with the quality of reproduction. Once the samples have been stored, the computer can recreate the original waveform by sequentially sending the stored values to a digital-to-analogue (D/A) converter at the same rate as the original sampling.

For speech reproduction a sampling rate of around 6 or 8 kHz is required. Using an 8-bit A/D converter, this results in a data rate of 8×8000 bits per second (bps). Thus the computer could only store about 10 seconds of speech in its 64K byte memory. Methods of data compression are therefore needed in order to reduce the data rate.

Delta Modulation

Rather than storing an 8-bit quantity for each sample, a delta modulator stores only a single bit. When data is collected from the A/D converter, the computer

178

compares the current reading to the preceding sample. If the value of the new sample is greater, then the computer stores a bit value of 1; otherwise a value of 0 will be stored.

This technique has the limitation that the sampling rate at which data is taken must be sufficiently fast that no significant information is lost from the input signal.

Differential Pulse Code Modulation

Like delta modulation, this technique stores the variation between samples, but allows more than a single bit of difference between samples. Thus more variation in the input signal is possible before severe distortion sets in, and so the sample rate is reduced.

Adaptive Differential Pulse Code Modulation (ADPCM)

ADPCM improves upon the other modulation techniques by dynamically varying the quantization between samples depending upon their rate of change while maintaining a low bit rate, condensing 12-bit PCM samples into 3 or 4 bits. The process that encodes/decodes each sample is complicated. A number of integrated circuits are produced that perform both storing and reproducing of digitized speech using the ADPCM encoding/decoding technique.

17.2 SIRIUS AUDIO SUBSYSTEM

Figure 17.1 is a block diagram of the ACT audio subsystem. The synchronous serial data adaptor (SSDA) accepts the sound bytes from the processor and puts out a serial bit data stream to the coder/decoder (CODEC), which uses a continuously-variable-slope delta modulator (CVSD) technique. It is then filtered by a low-pass filter in order to remove any high-frequency elements produced by the conversion. The volume-control section switches the analogue signal at a variable on–off rate, allowing the sound level to be controlled. The

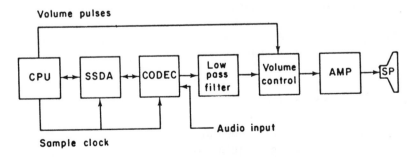

17.1 ACT Sirius audio subsystem.

180

analogue signal is finally sent through the audio amplifier to the speaker in the processor unit.

CVSD

Continuously-variable-slope delta modulation (CVDS) is the data reduction technique employed by the coder/decoder (CODEC) circuit.

Like the ADPCM Technique, this process assumes that the input signal's waveform has a fairly uniform and predictable slope. The CVSD circuitry provides increased dynamic range by adjusting the gain of the integrator. If the external algorithm indicates that the gain of the integrator is too small, the circuitry will modify the gain automatically.

The delta modulator encoder/decoder with the CVSD algorithm provides an efficient method for digitizing voice signals. It is useful for producing a few sound instructions to support on-screen activities by the Sirius. Each second of speech requires 2K bytes of storage.

17.3 GENERATION OF TONE

Although it is very difficult to program one's own voice vocabulary without the voice package, it is possible to experiment with the audio subsystem to produce simple tones.

Initialization of CODEC

During a power-up sequence, the system resets the audio subsystem in an internally-latched reset condition to prevent erroneous output transitions. The SSDA registers must be set before data is transmitted. SSDA registers are memory-mapped into absolute memory address 0e8060h–0e8061h, and the CODEC registers are at memory address 0e8080h–0e808fh.

```
;
;            ACT sirius audio subsystem
;
;            initialize SSDA/CODEC registers
;
audioinit  proc      near
           mov       ax,0e800h
           mov       es,ax                    ;0e800h → es
;
;            set SSDA registers
;
           mov       byte ptr es:[60h],0
           mov       byte ptr es:[61h],5eh
           mov       byte ptr es:[60h],40h
```

```
        mov         byte ptr es:[61h],0dh
        mov         byte ptr es:[60h],80h
        mov         byte ptr es:[61h],0aah
        mov         byte ptr es:[60h],0c0h
;
;       set CODEC
;
        mov         byte ptr es:[8bh],0c0h
        mov         byte ptr es:[84h],12h
;
;       set volume control
;
        mov         byte ptr es:[2bh],10h
        mov         byte ptr es:[2ah],0fh
        mov         byte ptr es:[28h],01h
        mov         byte ptr es:[4ch],0efh
        ret
audioinit   endp
```

There are nine volume levels that can be software selected:

```
audiovol            proc   near
;
;       on entry ax:  0 - 8
;                     0 - highest
;
        mov         si,ax               ;ax → si
        mov         ax,0e800h
        mov         es,ax               ;0e800h → es
;
        mov         al,volumetbl[si]
        mov         es:[2ah],al
        ret
volumetbl   db      0ffh,7fh,3fh,1fh,0fh,7,3,1,0

audiovol    endp
```

To generate different tone on the system, the following programs are used to examine the change in frequency produced when the various values of length, pitch, and type are set:

```
        .radix      16
        extrn       pnum:far            ;get number from keyboard
        extrn       gnum:far            ;output number
        extrn       pstg:far            ;output string
        extrn       pline:far           ;output cr,lf
```

```
voc         segment
            assume cs:voc,ds:voc,ss:stack
;
;           macro definition
;
M__STG      macro stg
            local   message,l__out             ;;display message on screen
            jmp     l__out
message     db      '&stg',0                    ;;define message
l__out:     mov     dx,offset message
            call    pstg
            endm                                ;;end macro
;
go:         mov     ax,voc
            mov     ds,ax                       ;init ds
            mov     ax,stack
            mov     ss,ax                       ;init ss
            mov     sp,offset s__data           ;set stack pointer
;
;           set SSDA/CODEC registers
;
            mov     ax,0e800                    ;memory mapped i/o ports
            mov     es,ax                       ;0e800h → es
            mov     byte ptr es:[60],0
            mov     byte ptr es:[61],5e
            mov     byte ptr es:[60],40
            mov     byte ptr es:[61],0dh
            mov     byte ptr es:[60],80
            mov     byte ptr es:[61],0aa
            mov     byte ptr es:[60],0c0
            mov     byte ptr es:[8bh],0c0       ;codec$ctl
            mov     byte ptr es:[84],12         ;codec$clk
;
            mov     byte ptr es:[2bh],10        ;vol$ctl
            mov     byte ptr es:[2a],0f         ;volume
            mov     word ptr es:[28],01         ;vol$clk
            and     byte ptr es:[4c],0ef
;
sound:      M__STG  ⟨enter type⟩
            call    gnum
            mov     dtype,ax                    ;input dtype
            M__STG  ⟨enter length⟩
            call    gnum
            mov     dlength,ax                  ;input dlength
            M__STG  ⟨enter pitch⟩
```

```
        call    gnum
        mov     pitch,ax                ;input pitch
        mov     cx,16                   ;generate 16 different
;                                       ;pitch
l__main: push   cx
        M__STG ⟨picth = ⟩
        mov     ax,pitch
        call    pnum                    ;output pitch
        call    pline
;
        mov     cx,dlength
        mov     ax,dtype
;
delay:  mov     dx,pitch
wait:   dec     dx
        jnz     wait
        mov     es:[61],al              ;output data to audio
        loop    short delay             ;port
;
        inc     pitch                   ;next tone up?
        pop     cx
        loop    l__main                 ;repeat
        jmp     sound                   ;ask for a different
;                                       ;pitch to try
;       dvoice                          ;⟨ctrl c⟩ to exit
;
pitch   dw      0
dlength dw      0
dtype   dw      0
voc     ends
;
stack   segmentstack
        db      128 dup(?)
s__data equ     $
stack   ends
        end     go


;
;       This program accepts key from 0 to 9 and generates
;       different tone
;
        .radix  16
        extrn   gnum:far                ;input number
        extrn   pnum:far                ;output number
        extrn   pstg:far                ;output string
```

```
                extrn    pline:far                    ;output newline
voc             segment
                assume cs:voc,ds:voc,ss:stack
;
go:             mov      ax,voc
                mov      ds,ax                        ;init ds
                mov      ax,stack
                mov      ss,ax                        ;init ss
                mov      sp,offset s__data            ;set stack pointer
;
;               set SSDA registers
;
                mov      ax,0e800                     ;memory mapped i/o ports
                mov      es,ax                        ;0e800h → es
                mov      byte ptr es:[60],0
                mov      byte ptr es:[61],5e
                mov      byte ptr es:[60],40
                mov      byte ptr es:[61],0dh
                mov      byte ptr es:[60],80
                mov      byte ptr es:[61],0aa
                mov      byte ptr es:[60],0c0
;
;               set CODEC
;
                mov      byte ptr es:[8bh],0c0        ;codec$ctl
                mov      byte ptr es:[84],12          ;codec$clk
                mov      byte ptr es:[2bh],10         ;vol$ctl
                mov      byte ptr es:[2a],0f          ;volume
                mov      word ptr es:[28],01          ;vol$clk
                and      byte ptr es:[4c],0ef
;
l__main:        mov      ah,8                         ;accept key without echo
                int      21h
                cmp      al,'0'                       ;only accept between '0'
                jl       l__main
                cmp      al,'9'                       ;and '9'
                jg       l__main
;
                sub      al,30h
                cbw                                   ;convert to binary in ax
                shl      ax,1                         ;ax * 2 → ax
                mov      bx,offset pitchtb            beginning of pitch table
                add      bx,ax                        ;calc address with displacement
                mov      ax,[bx]                      ;get data
                mov      pitch,ax                     ;store in pitch
```

```
                mov       volume, 0f          ;start loud
lp__main:       mov       al,volume
                mov       es:[2a],al          ;set volume
;
l__tune:        mov       cx,dlength          ;uses fixed length
                mov       ax,dtype            ;and type
delay:          mov       dx,pitch            ;pitch from pitch table
wait:           dec       dx
                jnz       wait
                mov       es:[61],al          ;output to audio
                loop      short delay         ;port
                stc
                rcl       volume,1            ;alter volume
                jp        l__main
;
                jmp       l__main
;
volumn          db        0a
pitch           dw        25d
dlength         dw        400d
dtype           dw        0d
pitchtb         dw        70d,72d,74d,86d,78d,180d,192d,84d,206d,88d
voc             ends
;
;               stack
;
stack           segment   stack
                db        128 dup(?)
s__data         equ       $
stack           ends
                end       go
```

CHAPTER 18

High-Resolution Graphics

The Sirius 1 display hardware has a bit-mapped high-resolution mode configured for 800 by 400 dots of bit-addressable display. In this chapter, the procedures required in switching the system into and out of hi-res mode (HIRES) is described. Routines for line and arc drawings are included as examples; the algorithms can be found elsewhere.* These routines can be used to provide the bases for a graphics package.

18.1 INITIALIZE HIRES MODE

In this mode, the reserve video, high/low intensity, and nondisplay attributes apply to fixed 16 by 16 dot cells on the screen, and the underline attribute is disabled.

To use the bit-mapped display mode, the CRT chip needs to be programmed, i.e. the output control line (HIRES) needs to be set. The screen buffer is then filled with pointers which address successive memory locations. The entire screen is set as 20000 contiguous words of bit-mapped dots organized into 16-bit wide columns, going from top to bottom and left to right as word addresses increase (Figure 18.1).

18.1 High-resolution display format.

---

*Newman, W. M. and Sproull, R. F. (1979). *Principles of Interactive Computer Graphics*, 2nd edn. McGraw-Hill, New York.

```
;
;              module name:-   dinit
;
;              function :-   this procedure sets ACT screen to hires mode
;
;              on entry    none
;              exit        none (reg destory)
;
dinit          proc        near
;
               mov         ax,0e000h              ;CRT controller port address
               mov         es,ax                  ; → es
;
;              program the CRT chip for bit-mapped display mode
;
               mov         si,offset crtc         ;crtc programming data
               mov         cx,10h                 ;16 word
               cld                                ;clear direction flag
crc:           lodsw                              ;ax:=[si]
               mov         es:[8000h],ax          ;ctrc port address
               loop        crc                    ;repeat until cx = 0
;
;              load screen base address f0000 with pointer table
;
               mov         ax0f000h               ;screen base addr
               mov         es,ax
               mov         bx,0                   ;buffer ptr → bx
               mov         ch,50                  ;50 columns
               mov         ax,4100h               ;normal brightness
fouter:        mov         cl,25                  ;25 rows per column
finner:        mov         es:[bx],ax             ;set pointer
               inc         ax                     ;next
               add         bx,100                 ;50 columns in word mode
               dec         cl                     ;cl–1 → cl
               jg          finner                 ;loop until cl = 0
               sub         bx,1249                ;50 * 25 – 1
               dec         ch                     ;ch–1 → ch
               jg          fouter                 ;loop until ch = 0
               ret
dinit          endp
```

```
;
;
;               recommended values for CRTC register initialization
;               (see ACT hardware reference manual p. 99)
;
                .radix    16
crtc            db        00,3a,01,32,02,34,03,0c9
                db        04,19,05,06,06,19,07,19
                db        08,03,09,0e,0a,20,0bh,0f
                db        0c,20,0dh,00,0e,00,0f,00
```

To reset to character display mode, use an ESC sequence provided:

ESC 'z' ESC 'E'

```
dexit           proc      near
                mov       ah,9                    ;msdos fn id for output string
                mov       dx,offset home          ;address of message → dx
                int       21h                     ;msdos entry point
                ret
dexit           endp
home            db        ESC,'z',ESC,'E',0,0,'$'
```

To clear the screen;

```
;
dclear          proc      near
;
;               clear screen when in hires mode begin at 2000h for 2000
;
;               entry:    none
;               exit:     no change
;
                push      ax                      ;save some of the regs
                push      cx
                push      es
                mov       ax,200h                 ;base of display bit map
                mov       es,ax                   ;init es
                mov       di,0                    ;0 → di
                mov       cx,2000                 ;count → 2000
                mov       ax,0                    ;0 → ax
                rep       stosw                   ;0 → es:di for 2000
```

```
;
            pop       es              ;restore
            pop       cx              ;   regs
            pop       ax
            ret
dclear      endp
```

18.2 DISPLAY PIXEL

Once the display is set in HIRES mode, to set or clear a dot (pixel) on the screen it is necessary to set or clear the corresponding bit of the display memory:

```
;
dpixel      proc                  near
;
;           module name:-     dpixel
;
;           function :-       this procedure sets pixel (dx,bx) to 1
;
;           on entry :-       dx = column
;                             bx = row
;
;           exit :-           di = address
;                             set pixel on screen
;
            push      ax              ;save registers
            push      bx
            push      cx
            push      dx
;
;           calculate word/bit position from column and row
;
            mov       cx,dx           ;column
            and       dx,0fff0h       ;(column/16)  *  16 → dx
            xor       cx,dx           ;column mod 16 → cx
;
            mov       ax,25           ;25 → ax
            mul       dx              ;column * 25
            add       ax,bx           ;+row
            shl       ax,1            ;*2 word mode
;
            mov       di,1
            rol       di,cl
```

```
            xchg        ax,di
            or          es:[di],ax              ;set the bit
;

            pop         dx                      ;restore regs.
            pop         cx
            pop         bx
            pop         ax
            ret
dpixel      endp
;
derase      proc                    near
;
;           module name :-  derase
;
;           function :-         clear pixel (dx,bx)
;
;           on entry:-          dx = column
;                               bx = row
;
;           exit :-             di = address
;                               clear pixel on screen
;
            push        ax                      ;save regs.
            push        bx
            push        cx
            push        dx
;
;           calculate word/bit position from column and row
;
            mov         cx,dx                   ;load column
            and         dx,0fff0h               ;dx most sign 3 byte
            xor         cx,dx                   ;column mod 16 → cx
;
            mov         ax,25
            mul         dx                      ;column * 25
            add         ax,bx                   ;+ row
            shl         ax,1                    ;*2
;
            mov         di,1
            rol         di,cl
            xchg        ax,di
            not         ax
```

```
        and      es:[di],ax              ;clear bit
;
        pop      dx                      ;restore regs
        pop      cx
        pop      bx
        pop      ax
        ret
derase  endp
```

18.3 LINE-DRAWING ALGORITHM

Straight-line segments are commonly used in graphics. There are therefore a great many algorithms written for generation of lines given the two endpoints. The digital differential analyser (DDA) generates lines from their differential equations. In each iteration, one of the coordinate values is inc/dec by 1, while the other coordinate may or may not change:

```
;
;
;              module name:-      dline
;
;              function :-        this procedure joins the two
;                                 co-ord pairs on screen.
;
;
;              on entry:-
;                sp+10 –          linetype
;                sp+8 –           final y co-ord
;                sp+6 –           final x co-ord
;                sp+4 –           initial y co-ord
;                sp+2 –           initial x co-ord
;                sp    –          return address
;
;              exit :-            none
;
;              extrn              dpixel:near
;
;              define arguments on stack
;
;
line__type  equ     word ptr [bp+20]
fyc         equ     word ptr [bp+18]
fxc         equ     word ptr [bp+16]
iyc         equ     word ptr [bp+14]
ixc         equ     word ptr [bp+12]
```

```
;
;               defines locals on stack
;
abs__delx     equ          word ptr [bp−2]
abs__dely     equ          word ptr [bp−4]
t__j          equ          word ptr [bp−6]
t__m          equ          word ptr [bp−8]
t__n          equ          word ptr [bp−10]
t__k          equ          word ptr [bp−12]
t__lv         equ          word ptr [bp−14]
t__d          equ          word ptr [bp−16]
step          equ          word ptr [bp−18]
vecdir        equ          byte ptr [bp−20]
t__t1         equ          byte ptr [bp−21]
t__t2         equ          byte ptr [bp−22]
;
dline         proc         near              ;define dline as near
;
;               save all registers used
;
              push         bp                ;save regs
              push         ax
              push         bx
              push         cx
              push         dx
              mov          bp,sp             ;bp points to local stack
              sub          sp,22             ;12 local variables on stack
;
;               line__type defines a mask for plotting
;
              mov          ax,line__type
              cmp          al,0              ;if linetype = 0
              jne          10__case1
              mov          dx,0ffffh         ;solid line
              jmp          10__endcase
10__case1     label        near
              cmp          al,1              ;if linetype = 1
              jne          10__case2
              mov          dx,0eeeeh         ;long dashed
              jmp          10__endcase
10__case2     label        near
              cmp          al,2              ;if linetype = 2
              jne          10__case3
              mov          dx,06666h         ;short dashed
              jmp          10__endcase
```

```
10__case3     label      near
              cmp        al,3                      ;if linetype = 3
              jne        10__default
              mov        dx,0aaaah                 ;dotted
              jmp        10__endcase
10__default   label      near
              mov        dx,0ffffh                 ;default = 0
10__endcase   label      near
              mov        step,dx                   ;mask → step
;
;                        begin line drawing
;
              mov        ax,fyc
              mov        bx,fxc
              mov        cx,iyc
              mov        dx,ixc                    ;load arguments
;
;                        adjust initial and final x,y co-ord
;                        such that x co-ord starts from a smaller value
;
              sub        bx,dx
              jnc        l__cpx
              neg        bx
l__cpx:       mov        abs__delx,bx              ;abs delx
;
              sub        ax,cx
              jnc        l__cpy
              neg        ax
;
              mov        dx,ixc
              mov        cx,fxc
              mov        ixc,cx
              mov        fxc,dx                    ;swap xc
;
              mov        dx,iyc
              mov        cx,fyc
              mov        iyc,cx
              mov        fyc,dx                    ;swap yc
;
l__cpy:       mov        abs__dely,ax              ;abs__dely
;
;                        determine the vector direction, vecdir
;
              mov        cx,fxc
              mov        vecdir,0                  ;0 → vecdir
```

```
                cmp         cx,ixc
                jge         l__ccx
                mov         vecdir,2                    ;2 → vecdir
;
l__ccx:         mov         cx,abs__delx
                mov         dx,abs__dely
                cmp         cx,dx
                jge         l__jmn
;
;               set constants
;
                mov         t__j,dx
                mov         t__m,dx
                mov         t__n,cx
                inc         vecdir
                jmp         l__jmn2
;
l__jmn:         mov         t__j,cx                     ;abs delx
                mov         t__m,cx
                mov         t__n,dx                     ;abs dely
;
;               set type of movement to draw
;               based on vecdir
;
l__jmn2:        mov         al,vecdir
                cmp         al,0
                jne         l__case1
                mov         t__t1,0
                mov         t__t2,1
                jmp         l__precalc
;
l__case1:       cmp         al,1
                jne         l__case2
                mov         t__t1,2
                mov         t__t2,1
                jmp         l__precalc
;
l__case2:       cmp         al,2
                jne         l__case3
                mov         t__t1,4
                mov         t__t2,3
                jmp         l__precalc
;
l__case3:       cmp         al,3
                jne         l__precalc                  ;no default case
```

```
            mov     t__t1,2
            mov     t__t2,3
;
l__precalc  label   near
            mov     ax,t__n
            shl     ax,1                ;   2 * n
            mov     t__k,ax             ;k = n + n
            mov     bx,t__m
            shl     bx,1                ;   2 * m
            sub     ax,bx               ;k − (m+m)
            mov     t__lv,ax            ;lv = k − (m+m)
            add     ax,t__m             ;lv + m
            mov     t__d,ax             ;d = lv + m
;
;           set the points on the graphic plane
;           dx :-   xaddr
;           bx :-   yaddr
;
            mov     bx,iyc
            mov     dx,ixc
            mov     cx,t__j
;
l__set__pixel label  near
            push    cx                  ;save loop count
            mov     cx,step
            ror     cx,1                ;mask rotate right 1 bit;
            mov     step,cx
            test    cx,1
            jz      no__plot
            call    dpixel              ;set pixel
;
no__plot:   cmp     ax,0                ;if d < 0
            jge     l__d6
            add     ax,t__k
            mov     cl,t__t1
            cmp     cl,4                ;if t1 == 4
            jne     l__d2
            dec     dx                  ;xaddr − −
            jmp     l__da
l__d2:      cmp     cl,0                ;if t1 == 0
            jne     l__d4
            inc     dx                  ;xaddr ++
            jmp     l__da
l__d4:      inc     bx                  ;yaddr ++
            jmp     l__da
```

```
;
l__d6:      add       ax,t__lv              ;d += lv
            mov       cl,t__t2
            cmp       cl,1                  ;if t2 == 1
            jne       l__d8
            inc       dx                    ;xaddr ++
            inc       bx                    ;yaddr ++
            jmp       l__da
l__d8:      dec       dx                    ;xaddr --
            inc       bx                    ;yaddr ++
l__da:      pop       cx
            loop      l__set__pixel         ;main loop
;
;           restore registers
;
            mov       sp,bp
            pop       dx
            pop       cx
            pop       bx
            pop       ax
            pop       bp
;
            ret       10                    ;5 arguments
dline       endp
```

Examples using dline:

```
            extrn     dinit:near
            extrn     dclear:near
            extrn     delay:near
            extrn     dline:near
;
;           display lines across that screen
;
draw        segment   public
            assume cs:draw,ds:draw,ss:stack
go:         mov       ax,draw
            mov       ds,ax                 ;init ds
            mov       ax,stack
            mov       ss,ax                 ;init ss
            mov       sp,offset s__data     ;set stack pointer
;
            call      dinit
;
main__lp:   call      dclear                ;clear screen
```

```
                mov      ax,0
                mov      ixc,ax
                mov      iyc,ax                ;top left hand corner
                mov      ax,799
                mov      fxc,ax
                mov      ax,399
                mov      fyc,ax                ;bottom right
;
;               draw lines across the screen
;
                mov      cx,799
l__in:          push     cx
                push     linetype
                push     fyc
                push     fxc
                push     iyc
                push     ixc                   ;all arguments on stack
                call     dline                 ;draw line
;
                inc      ixc                   ;horizontally
                dec      fxc                   ;next line
                pop      cx
                loop     l__in                 ;loop until cx = 0
                call     delay
;
                inc      linetype              ;nextline type
                and      linetype,3
                jmp      main__lp
;
;               data area
;
fxc             dw       799
fyc             dw       399
ixc             dw       0
iyc             dw       0
linetype        dw       2
draw            ends
;
;               stack
;
stack           segment  stack
                db       128 dup(?)
s__data         equ      $
stack           ends
                end      go
```

The program is linked with

LINK DRAW+DINIT+DLINE/HIGH

to save the lower memory for the screen bit-map.

Both curves and histograms can be drawn using the dline procedure:

```
;
dhisto          proc        near
;
;               display histogram
;
;               entry       bx  -   array of data points
;                                   offset 0 = init x
;                                          1 = x inc
;                                          2 = ymin
;                                          3 = ys
;                           cx  -   number of data points
;
                public      dhisto
;
                push        ax                      ;save
                push        bx                      ;    all
                push        cx                      ;          general
                push        dx                      ;registers
;
                mov         dx,[bx]                 ;initial x value
                mov         ax,[bx+2]               ;x increment
                mov         xinc,ax
                mov         ax,[bx+4]               ;ymin
                mov         ymin,ax
                add         bx,6                    ;pointer to 1st data point
;
l_his:          push        cx
                mov         ax,0
                push        ax                      ;linetype = solid
                mov         ax,[bx]
                push        ax                      ;fy
                push        dx                      ;fx
                push        ymin                    ;iy
                push        dx                      ;ix
                call        dline                   ;left boundary
;
                mov         ax,0
```

```
        push    ax                  ;solid
        mov     ax,[bx]
        push    ax                  ;fy
        push    dx                  ;fx
        push    ax                  ;iy
        add     dx,xinc             ;next x
        push    dx                  ;ix
        call    dline               ;top line
;
        mov     ax,0
        push    ax                  ;solid
        mov     ax,[bx]
        push    ax                  ;fy
        push    dx                  ;fx
        push    ymin                ;iy
        push    dx                  ;ix
        call    dline               ;right boundary
;
        inc     bx                  ;next word
        inc     bx
        pop     cx
        loop    l__his              ;repeat for no of data points
;
;       return
;
        pop     dx                  ;restore regs
        pop     cx
        pop     bx
        pop     ax
        ret
dhisto  endp
;
;
dcurve  proc    near
;
;       display curve
;
;       entry   bx  -   array of data points
;                       offset 0 = init x
;                              1 = x inc
;                              2 = ys
;               ax  -   c__type
;               cx  -   no of data points
;
        public  dcurve
```

```
;
                push    ax                      ;save regs
                push    bx
                push    cx
                push    dx
;
                mov     c_type,ax               ;store in local
                mov     dx,[bx]                 ;init x
                mov     ax,[bx+2]               ;x inc
                mov     xinc,ax
                add     bx,4
l_v2:           push    c_type                  ;type
                mov     ax,[bx]
                push    ax                      ;fy
                push    dx                      ;fx
                inc     bx
                inc     bx
                mov     ax,[bx]                 ;
                push    ax                      ;iy
                add     dx,xinc
                push    dx                      ;ix
                call    dline                   ;joins two points
                loop    l_v2                    ;repeat until all points
;
;               return
;
                pop     dx                      ;retrieve regs
                pop     cx
                pop     bx
                pop     ax
                ret
dcurve          endp
;
;               predefined data
;
c_type          dw      0                       ;local data on stack
xinc            dw      0                       ;no re-entrance
ymin            dw      0
```

18.4 DRAW ARCS

A circular arc is required in drawing a pie chart. This algorithm uses an approximation method in determining the next position on the arc in a counter-clockwise direction.

In order that the circular arc appears as defined, it is necessary to scale the x,y axis as x:y = 3:2:

```
;
;                       module name :- darc
;
;
;                       function :- this procedure joins the two
;                                   co-ord pairs with an arc at
;                                   centre xc,yc on screen.
;
;                       on entry:-
;                           sp+12 - final y co-ord (rel to centre)
;                           sp+10 - final x co-ord
;                           sp+8  - initial y co-ord
;                           sp+6  - initial x co-ord
;                           sp+4  - centre y co-ord (absolute)
;                           sp+2  - centre x co-ord
;                           sp    - return address
;
;                       exit :- none
;
;                       extrn   dpixel:near
;
;                       define arguments on stack
;
yc              equ         word ptr [bp+14]
ixc             equ         word ptr [bp+16]
iyc             equ         word ptr [bp+18]
fxc             equ         word ptr [bp+20]
fyc             equ         word ptr [bp+22]
;
;                       define locals on stack
;
t__dir          equ         word ptr [bp-2]
t__dir1         equ         word ptr [bp-4]
t__syfinal      equ         word ptr [bp-6]
t__z            equ         word ptr [bp-8]
t__z1           equ         word ptr [bp-10]
t__z2           equ         word ptr [bp-12]
t__dir2         equ         word ptr [bp-14]
;
darc            proc        near                    ;define dline as near
;
                push        bp                      ;save bp
                push        ax
                push        bx
```

```
        push    cx
        push    dx
        mov     bp,sp
        sub     sp,14           ;sp = last local var
;
;       retrieve arguments on stack
;
        mov     bx,iyc
        mov     dx,ixc
;
;       determine initial direction
;
;       dx :-   xaddr
;       bx :-   yaddr
;       ax :-   dir
;
        cmp     bx,0
        jge     l__c0
        neg     bx
l__c0:  shl     dx,1            ;x = 2 * x
        cmp     dx,0            ;if x > 0
        jge     l__c2
        neg     dx
l__c2:  cmp     bx,dx           ;abs(y) >x abs(2x)
        jle     l__d0
        mov     bx,iyc
        cmp     bx,0
        jge     l__C4
        mov     ax,0            ;dir = 0
        jmp     l__f6
l__C4:  mov     ax,4            ;dir = 4
        jmp     l__f6
;
l__d0:  sar     dx,1
        sar     dx,1            ;x/2
        cmp     bx,dx           ;abs(y) > abs(x/2)
        jge     l__e0
        mov     bx,iyc
        cmp     bx,0            ;if y > 0
        jl      l__d2
        mov     ax,6            ;dir = 6
        jmp     l__f6
l__d2:  mov     ax,2            ;dir = 2
        jmp     l__f6
;
```

```
l__e0:          mov        bx,iyc
                mov        dx,ixc
                cmp        bx,0                ;if y > 0
                jl         l__f0
                cmp        dx,0                ;if x > 0
                jl         l__e2
                mov        ax,5                ;dir = 5
                jmp        l__f6
l__e2:          mov        ax,7                ;dir = 7
                jmp        l__f6
;
l__f0:          cmp        dx,0                ;if x > 0
                jl         l__f2
                mov        ax,3                ;dir = 3
                jmp        l__f6
l__f2:          mov        ax,1                ;dir = 1
l__f6:          mov        t__dir,ax           ;store dir for later use
;
;               set syfinal = sign of yfinal
;
                mov        cx,1                ;sign = +ve
                mov        ax,fyc
                cmp        ax,0
                jg         l__f8
                neg        cx                  ;sign = −1
l__f8:          mov        t__syfinal,cx       ;store syfinal
;
;               main loop to generate next point
;               by successive approximation
;
                mov        dx,ixc
                mov        bx,iyc
l__loop         label      near
;
                push       dx
                push       bx
                mov        ax,dx               ;keep a copy of x
                shl        dx,1                ;2*x
                add        dx,ax               ;3*x
                sar        dx,1                ;1.5x
                add        dx,xc
                add        bx,yc
                call       dpixel              ;plot the point
                pop        bx
                pop        dx
```

```
;
;                   next point
;

                   push      t__dir              ;arg dir
                   push      t__z                ;arg z
                   push      bx                  ;arg y
                   push      dx                  ;arg x
                   call      dnext
                   mov       t__z1,ax            ;return in ax
                   cmp       ax,0
                   je        l__p8               ;got it
;
;                   prepare for second trial
;

                   mov       cx,t__dir           ;dir
                   cmp       ax,0
                   jle       l__n2
                   inc       cx                  ;dir + +
                   jmp       l__n4
l__n2:             dec       cx
l__n4:             and       cx,7                ;dir mod 7
                   mov       t__dir1,cx          ;dir1 = dir & 7
;
;                   second trial
;

                   push      cx                  ;arg dir1
                   push      t__z                ;arg z
                   push      bx                  ;arg y
                   push      dx                  ;arg x
                   call      dnext
                   mov       t__z2,ax            ;return in ax
;
;                   choose new direction with small
;                   absolute error
;

                   mov       ax,t__z1
                   cmp       ax,0
                   jg        l__p2
                   neg       ax                  ;abs(z1)
l__p2:             mov       cx,t__z2
                   cmp       cx,0
                   jg        l__p4
                   neg       cx                  ;abs(z2)
l__p4:             cmp       ax,cx               ;if(abs(z1) < abs(z2))
                   jl        l__p6
```

```
                mov     ax,t__dir1
                mov     t__dir,ax           ;dir = dir1
                mov     ax,t__z2
                jmp     l__p8
l__p6:          mov     ax,t__z1
l__p8:          mov     t__z,ax             ;z= z1 or z2
;
;               find new co-ord for x,y
;
;
                mov     cx,1                ;+ve sign
                mov     ax,t dir
                shl     ax,1                ;*2 word mode
                mov     si,ax
                add     dx,xdir[si]
                add     bx,ydir[si]
                jns     l__s0
                neg     cx                  ;sign = -1
l__s0:          cmp     cx,t__syfinal
                je      l__s2
                jmp     l__loop             ;repeat
l__s2:          cmp     dx,fxc
                je      l__s4
                jmp     l__loop             ;repeat
;
;               return
;
l__s4:          mov     sp,bp
                pop     dx
                pop     cx
                pop     bx
                pop     ax
                pop     bp
;
;               return to caller
;
                ret     12
darc            endp
;
;               module name :- dnext
;
;
;               function :- calculate difference between
;               x*x + y*y and x'*x' + y'*y'
;
;               on entry :-
;               sp+8 - direction
```

```
;               sp+6  –  error value
;               sp+4  –  current y co-ord
;               sp+2  –  current x co-rd
;               sp    –  return address
;
;               exit :-
;               ax  –   new error value
;
dnext           proc        near                    ;define dnext
;
;               define arguments on stack
;
nx              equ         word ptr [bp+10]
ny              equ         word ptr [bp+12]
nz              equ         word ptr [bp+14]
ndir            equ         word ptr [bp+16]
;
                push        bp                      ;save bp
                push        bx                      ;save
                push        cx                      ;all
                push        dx                      ;regs
                mov         bp,sp
;
;               retrieve arguments on stack
;
                mov         ax,ndir                 ;direction
                mov         bx,ny                   ;y value
                mov         dx,nx                   ;x value
;
                mov         cx,0                    ;set nz to 0
                cmp         ax,1
                jne         l__case0
                shl         bx,1                    ;2*y
                inc         bx                      ;2*y + 1
                mov         cx,bx                   ;nz = 2*y + 1
                jmp         l__case01
;
l__case0:       cmp         ax,0
                jne         l__case3
l__case01       label       near
                shl         dx,1                    ;2*x
                inc         dx                      ;2*x + 1
                add         cx,dx                   ;nz + = 2*x + 1
                jmp         l__case__end
;
```

```
l_case3:      cmp      ax,3
              jne      l_case2
              shl      dx,1              ;2*x
              neg      dx               ;-2*x
              inc      dx               ;1-2*x
              mov      cx,dx            ;nz = 1 - 2*x
              jmp      l_case21
;
l_case2:      cmp      ax,2
              jne      l_case5
l_case21      label    near
              shl      bx,1             ;2*y
              inc      bx               ;2*y + 1
              add      cx,bx            ;nz + = 2*y + 1
              jmp      l_case_end
;
l_case5:      cmp      ax,5
              jne      l_case4
              shl      bx,1             ;2*y
              neg      bx               ;-2*y
              inc      bx               ;1 - 2*y
              mov      cx,bx            ;nz = 1 - 2*y
              jmp      l_case41
;
l_case4:      cmp      ax,4
              jne      l_case7
l_case41      label    near
              shl      dx,1             ;2*x
              neg      dx               ;-2*x
              inc      dx               ;1 - 2*x
              add      cx,dx
              jmp      l_case_end
;
l_case7:      cmp      ax,7
              jne      l_case6
              shl      dx,1             ;2*x
              inc      dx               ;1 + 2*x
              mov      cx,dx            ;nz = 1 + 2*x
              jmp      l_case61
;
l_case6:      cmp      ax,6
              jne      l_case_end
l_case61      label    near
              shl      bx,1             ;2*y
              neg      bx               ;-2*y
```

```
                inc         bx                      ;1 − 2*y
                add         cx,bx                   ;nz + = 1 − 2*y
;
l__case__end label          near
                add         cx,nz                   ;nz + = nz1
                mov         ax,cx
;
;               return
;
                mov         sp,bp
                pop         dx
                pop         cx
                pop         bx
                pop         bp
                ret         8
dnext           endp
;
;               temp data area
;
xdir            dw          1,1,0,−1,−1,−1,0,1
ydir            dw          0,1,1,1,0,−1,−1,−1
;
;               end of local data
;               end of module
;
```

Example of darc:

```
                extrn       dinit:near
                extrn       dclear:near
                extrn       dexit:near
                extrn       dline:near
                extrn       darc:near
;
draw            segment  public
                assume cs:draw,ds:draw,ss:stack
go:             mov         ax,draw
                mov         ds,ax                   ;init ds
                mov         ax,stack
                mov         ss,ax                   ;init ss
                mov         sp,offset s__data       ;set stack pointer
;
                call        dinit
;
main__lp:       call        dclear                  ;clear screen
```

```
;
              mov     ax,160         ;fy
              push    ax
              mov     ax,0           ;fx
              push    ax
              push    ax             ;iy
              mov     ax,-160
              push    ax             ;ix
              mov     ax,200
              push    ax             ;yc
              mov     ax,400
              push    ax
              call    darc
;
;       draw lines
;
              mov     ax,0
              push    ax             ;linetype = solid
              mov     ax,200
              push    ax
              mov     ax,160
              push    ax
              mov     ax,200
              push    ax
              mov     ax,400
              push    ax
              call    dline
;
              mov     ax,0
              push    ax             ;linetype = solid
              mov     ax,200
              push    ax
              mov     ax,400
              push    ax
              mov     ax,360
              push    ax
              mov     ax,400
              push    ax
              call    dline
;
              mov     ax,0
              push    ax
              mov     ax,-160
              push    ax
              mov     ax,160
```

```
                push    ax
                mov     ax,0
                push    ax
                mov     ax,230
                push    ax
                mov     ax,370
                push    ax
                call    darc
;
                mov     ax,0
                push    ax
                mov     ax,230
                push    ax
                mov     ax,130
                push    ax
                mov     ax,230
                push    ax
                mov     ax,370
                push    ax
                call    dline
;
                mov     ax,0
                push    ax
                mov     ax,230
                push    ax
                mov     ax,370
                push    ax
                mov     ax,390
                push    ax
                mov     ax,370
                push    ax
                call    dline           ;final boundary
;
l__rep:         mov     ah,6
                mov     dl,0ffh
                int     21h             ;wait for keyboard interupt
                cmp     al,0
                jz      l__rep
                call    dexit
                int     23h             ;return to msdos
;
draw            ends
;
;               stack
;
```

```
stack           segment stack
                db          128 dup(?)
s__data         equ         $
stack           ends
                end         go
```

18.5 DRAW CHARACTERS

To display characters in hi-res mode, it is necessary to set each individual pixel as defined in the font cell.

Dchar uses the font table in the original ACT font table, and can display different size characters:

```
;
;               module name :- dchar
;
;               function :- this procedure draws an ascii character
;                           at position x,y
;
;               on entry :-
;                   sp      - return address
;                   sp+2    - ascii char
;                   sp+6    - x
;                   sp+8    - y
;                   sp+10   - type 1 horz
;                                 2 vert
;                   sp+12   - size
;
;               exit :- none
;
                extrn       dpixel:near
                extrn       derase:near
                public      dchar
;
draw            segment     public
                assume cs:draw,ds:draw
;
;               define arguments on stack
;
c__size         equ         word ptr [bp+20]
c__type         equ         word ptr [bp+18]
yc              equ         word ptr [bp+16]
xc              equ         word ptr [bp+14]
char            equ         word ptr [bp+12]
```

```
;
;             save registers
;
dchar        proc      near
             push      bp                  ;save all regs
             push      ax
             push      bx
             push      cx
             push      dx
             mov       bp,sp               ;bp points to local stack
;
             mov       ax,char             ;load char
             add       ax,44h              ;offset from top
             mov       dl,20h              ;32 byte each
             mul       dl                  ;calc offset from top
             mov       bx,ax               ;1st byte of char font
;
             mov       cx,16               ;set of loop count = 16
             cmp       c__type,1           ;type of char display
             jnz       dside               ;sideway
;
l__01:       push      cx                  ;16 rows
             push      bx
             push      dx
             mov       ax,40h              ;base of font table
             mov       es,ax               ;es = 40h
             mov       ax,es:[bx]          ;load font pattern
             mov       dx,200h             ;base of bit-map
             mov       es,dx               ;es = 200h
             mov       cx,10               ;10 columns
             mov       bx,0001h            ;mask
             mov       dx,xc               ;start column address
;
l__02:       push      cx                  ;save regs
             push      ax
             push      bx
             test      ax,bx               ;is bit set
;
             mov       bx,yc               ;row → bx
             jz        l__erase            ;clear bit
             cmp       c__size,1           ;if char size not eq 1
             jnz       l__exp              ;jump to l__exp
             call      dpixel              ;set pixel
             jmp       l__cont             ;next bit
;
```

```
;               expand each bit into a square block
;
l__exp:    mov       ax,1
           mov       cx,c__size
           call      dxpand
           jmp       l__cont
;
;               erase each bit
;
l__erase:  cmp       c__size,1
           jnz       l__exp2
           call      derase
           jmp       l__cont
;
l__exp2:   mov       ax,0
           mov       cx,c__size
           call      dxpand            ;clear square block
l__cont:   pop       bx
           shl       bx,1
           add       dx,c__size
           pop       ax
           pop       cx
           loop      l__02             ;repeat for 10
;
           pop       dx
           pop       bx
           mov       ax,c__size
           add       yc,ax             ;next row
           inc       bx
           inc       bx                ;next word
           pop       cx
           loop      l__01             ;repeat for 16
           jmp       l__exit
;
;               display char vertically
;               no check on size
;
dside      label     near
ld__01:    push      cx                ;16 rows
           push      bx
           push      dx
           mov       ax,40h
           mov       es,ax             ;es = 40h
           mov       ax,es:[bx]        ;load font pattern
           mov       dx,200h
```

```
                    mov       es,dx              ;es = 200h
                    mov       cx,10              ;16 columns
                    mov       dx,0200h           ;mask
                    mov       bx,yc
;
ld__02:             push      cx
                    push      dx
                    test      ax,dx              ;is bit set
;
                    mov       dx,xc
                    jz        ld__erase
                    call      dpixel
                    jmp       ld__cont
ld__erase:          call      derase
ld__cont:           pop       dx
                    shr       dx,1
                    inc       bx
                    pop       cx
                    loop      ld__02
;
                    pop       dx
                    pop       bx
                    inc       xc
                    inc       bx
                    inc       bx
                    pop       cx
                    loop      ld__01
;
l__exit:            mov       sp,bp              ;retrieve regs
                    pop       dx
                    pop       cx
                    pop       bx
                    pop       ax
                    pop       bp
                    ret       10                 ;return with stack pop
dchar               endp
;
;                   proc dxpand
;
;                   entry :-
;                       cx - c__size
;                       ax - 0 erase
;                               1 plot
;
dxpand              proc      near
```

```
                push       ax                          ;save regs
                push       bx
                push       cx
                push       dx
                mov        d__size,cx
;
l__x0:          push       cx                          ;save regs inside loop
                push       bx
                push       dx
;
                mov        cx,d__size
l__x2:          push       cx
                push       ax
                cmp        ax,0
                jnz        l__xplot
;               call       derase
                jmp        short  l__x4
l__xplot:       call       dpixel
l__x4:          inc        dx
                pop        ax
                pop        cx
                loop       short  l__x2        ;repeat
;
                pop        dx
                pop        bx
                inc        bx
                pop        cx
                loop       short  l__x0        ;repeat
;
                pop        dx                           ;retrieve regs
                pop        cx
                pop        bx
                pop        ax
                ret
d__size         dw         1
dxpand          endp
draw            ends
                end
```

18.6 MAKING A HARD COPY

Having been able to plot curves, pie charts, and characters on the screen, it is sometimes useful to have a hardcopy made. A few graphic plotters are available, but it is usually necessary to rely on a dot-matrix printer: most dot-matrix printers today have an option for printing graphics. Each line on

216

the printer can be represented by a number of vertical columns with six, seven, or even eight dot patterns. An EPSON FX-80 printer is used here to demonstrate the principle. Although the escape sequence to turn on the graphics mode is different for each model of printer, this procedure can readily be modified for the others.

With the EPSON FX-80 printer, under dual-density bit image mode, the maximum number of dots across the screen is 960. There are 8 dot wires in the print head, where a dot denotes the bit 1 and a blank denotes the bit 0.

The code setting the dual-density bit image is

   ESC,'L',n2,n1

where n2 and n1 are calculated as

   n2 = (Number of data) MOD 256

and n1 = INT (Number of data/256)

```
;
;                    screen dump to EPSON FX80
;
;                    module name :- Dfx80
;
;                    function :- this procedure dumps the screen data to printer
;
;                    on entry :-        none
;
;                    exit :- regs corrupted
;
                                  public     dfx80
ESC                               equ        1bh
LF                                equ        0ah
CR                                equ        0dh
PUTC                              equ        5
DOS                               equ        21h
EMPTY                             equ        0
BIT_PER_LINE                      equ        8           ;
WORD_PER_LINE                     equ        50          ;
LINE_PER_PAGE                     equ        50
TOTBIT_PER_LINE                   equ        800
P_SIZE                            equ        TOTBIT_PER_LINE
;
draw          segment    public
```

```
            assume    cs:draw,ds:draw
;
;           init printer to graphic mode
;
dfx80       proc      near
            mov       ah,PUTC
            mov       dl,ESC              ;esc
            int       DOS
            mov       ah,PUTC
            mov       dl,'1'              ;'1'
            int       DOS
;
;           main loop
;           start with si = 0
;
            mov       count,LINE__PER__PAGE
            mov       si,0
;
;           beginning of new pbuffer
;
l__10       label     near
;
;           load buffer with 0h
;
            push      es                  ;save es = 200
            les       di,pfptr            ;es:di = offset pbuffer
            mov       cx,p__size
            cld
            mov       al,EMPTY
            rep       stosb               ;repeat until all done
            pop       es
;
;           turn on normal graphic mode
;
            mov       ah,PUTC
            mov       dl,ESC
            int       DOS
            mov       ah,PUTC
            mov       dl,'L'
            int       DOS
            mov       ah,PUTC
            mov       dl,TOTBIT__PER__LINE mod 256
            int       DOS
            mov       ah,PUTC
            mov       dl,TOTBIT__PER__LINE / 256
```

```
                int         DOS
;
;               loop to generate pbuffer
;
                mov         dmask,80h                   ;most sign. bit
                mov         cx,BIT__PER__LINE
l__20:          push        cx
                push        si
                mov         di,offset pbuffer
                mov         cx,WORD__PER__LINE  ;16 * 50 = 800
;
;               loop to check each word in the line
;
l__30:          push        cx                          ;next loop count
                mov         dx,1                        ;mask
                mov         cx,16                       ;bits per word
                mov         ax,es:[si]                  ;load word
;
;               loop to check each bit in a word
;
l__40:          test        ax,dx                       ;check bit with mask in dx
                jz          l__42                       ;skip if not set
                mov         bl,dmask                    ;byte mode mask
                or          ds:[di],bl                  ;set bit in pbuffer
l__42:          shl         dx,1                        ;set next bit in mask
                inc         di                          ;next pbuffer byte
                loop        l__40
;
;               next word
;
                add         si,800                      ;next word in bitmap
                pop         cx
                loop        l__30                       ;loop until cx = 0
;
;               next line
;
                shr         dmask,1                     ;next bit in each line
                pop         si
                inc         si                          ;si go from 0 to 399
                inc         si
                pop         cx
                loop        l__20                       ;loop until cx = 0
;
;               print it out, and start again
;
```

```
                push       es
                push       si
                les        si,pfptr                    ;es:si = pbuffer
                mov        cx,p__size                  ;no of bytes
l__50:          lodsb
                mov        dl,al
                mov        ah,PUTC
                int        DOS
                loop       l__50
                pop        si
                pop        es
;
;               output linefeed
;
                mov        ah,PUTC
                mov        dl,CR
                int        DOS
                mov        ah,PUTC
                mov        dl,LF
                int        DOS
;
;               next line (8 bit) down the page
;
                dec        count
                jz         l__60
                jmp        l__10                       ;loop until count = 0
;
;               turn printer back to 10pci char mode
;
l__60:          mov        ah,PUTC
                mov        dl,ESC
                int        DOS
                mov        ah,PUTC
                mov        dl,'0'
                int        DOS
                ret                                    ;finish
count           dw         LINE__PER__PAGE
dmask           db         0
pfptr           dd         pbuffer
pbuffer         db         P__SIZE dup (EMPTY)
df×80           endp
;
draw            ends
                end
```

Finally, a complete program to display all the functions on the screen, and a hardcopy on the EPSON FX-80 printer (Figure 18.2).

The program is linked with

LINK DRAW+DINIT+DLINES+DARC+DCHAR+DFX80/high

```
;
;                       HIRES example, a complete screen
;
                extrn   dinit:near
                extrn   dclear:near
                extrn   dexit:near
                extrn   dline:near
                extrn   dhisto:near
                extrn   dcurve:near
                extrn   darc:near
                extrn   dchar:near
                extrn   dstg:near
                extrn   df×80:near
;
;                       macro definitions
;
M__LINE         macro       p__type,p__fy,p__fx,p__iy,p__ix
                mov         ax,p__type
                push        ax
                mov         ax,p__fy
                push        ax
                mov         ax,p__fx
                add         ax,XOFFSET
                push        ax
                mov         ax,p__iy
                push        ax
                mov         ax,p__ix
                add         ax,XOFFSET
                push        ax
                call        dline
                endm
;
M__ARC          macro       p__fy,p__fx,p__iy,p__ix,p__yc,p__xc
                mov         ax,p__fy
                push        ax
                mov         ax,p__fx
                push        ax
                mov         ax,p__iy
                push        ax
```

```
                mov      ax,p__ix
                push     ax
                mov      ax,p__yc
                push     ax
                mov      ax,p__xc
                add      ax,XOFFSET
                push     ax
                call     darc
                endm

;
M__CHAR         macro    p__size,p__type,p__chy,p__chx,p__char
                mov      ax,p__size
                push     ax                  ;c__size
                mov      ax,p__type
                push     ax                  ;c__type
                mov      ax,p__chy           ;start y co-ord
                push     ax
                mov      ax,p__chx           ;start x co-ord
                add      ax,XOFFSET
                push     ax
                mov      al,p__char
                push     ax                  ;ascii char
                call     dchar
                endm

;
M__HISTO        macro    p__array,p__length
                mov      bx,offset p__array
                mov      cx,p__length
                call     dhisto
                endm

;
M__CURVE        macro    p__array,p__length,p__type
                mov      bx,offset p__array
                mov      cx,p__length
                mov      ax,p__type
                call     dcurve
                endm

;
M__CIRCLE       macro    p__radius,p__yc,p__xc
                m__arc   p__radius,0,p__radius,0,p__yc,p__xc
                endm
```

```
;
M_STG         macro     p_size,p_type,p_chy,p_chx,p_stg
              local     l_start,l_label
              jmp       short l_start
l_label       db        '&p_stg',0              ;;stg defn
l_start:      mov       ax,p_size
              push      ax                     ;;c_size
              mov       ax,p_type
              push      ax                     ;;c_type
              mov       ax,p_chy               ;;start y co-ord
              push      ax
              mov       ax,p_chx               ;;start x co-ord
              add       ax,XOFFSET
              push      ax
              mov       ax,offset l_label
              push      ax                     ;;ascii char pointer
              call      dstg
              endm

;
;             equate symbols
;
SOLID         equ       0
BROKE         equ       1
VERT          equ       2
HORZ          equ       1
TIME1         equ       1
TIME2         equ       2
XOFFSET       equ       250

;
;             main program to display screen
;
draw          segment public
              assume cs:draw,ds:draw,ss:stack
go:           mov       ax,draw
              mov       ds,ax                  ;init ds
              mov       ax,stack
              mov       ss,ax                  ;init ss
              mov       sp,offset s_data       ;set stack pointer

;
              call      dinit                  ;set HIRES mode
              call      dclear                 ;clear screen
;
```

```
        M__ARC      60,0,0,-60,100,370          ;draw major arc
        M__LINE     SOLID,100,280,100,370       ;horz boundary
        M__LINE     SOLID,160,370,100,370       ;vert boundary
;
        M__ARC      0,-60,60,0,110,360          ;minor arc
        M__LINE     SOLID,110,270,110,360       ;horz boundary
        M__LINE     SOLID,110,360,170,360       ;vert boundary
;
        M__CIRCLE   75,100,370                  ;draw circle
;
        M__HISTO    harray,6
        M__LINE     SOLID,20,20,180,20          ;y axis
        M__LINE     SOLID,180,20,180,220        ;x axis
;
        M__CURVE    carray,10,SOLID             ;draw curves
        M__CURVE    cary2,10,BROKE
;
        M__LINE     SOLID,220,30,376,30         ;y axis
        M__LINE     SOLID,376,30,376,480        ;x axis
;
;       labels axes
;
        M__STG      TIME2,HORZ,10,150,⟨SAMPLE⟩
        M__STG      TIME1,HORZ,190,50,⟨Histogram⟩
        M__STG      TIME1,HORZ,190,300,⟨PIE CHART⟩
        M__STG      TIME1,HORZ,380,250,⟨X AXIS⟩
        m__STG      TIME1,VERT,330,10,⟨Y AXIS⟩
;
;       label curves
;
        M__CHAR     TIME1,HORZ,220,390,'C'
        M__CHAR     TIME1,HORZ,230,398,'1'
        M__CHAR     TIME1,HORZ,300,390,'C'
        M__CHAR     TIME1,HORZ,310,398,'2'
;
;       dump to printer
;
        call        dfx80
;
l__rep: mov         ah,6
        mov         dl,0ffh
        int         21h                         ;wait for keyboard interrupt
        cmp         al,0
        jz          l__rep
        call        dexit
        int         23h                         ;return to MSDOS
```

```
;
;               predefined data
;
harray      dw        20+XOFFSET,30,180
            dw        160,80,40,60,130,150,0
carray      dw        30+XOFFSET,40
            dw        250,270,320,300,320,250
            dw        300,260,240,230,220
cary2       dw        30+XOFFSET,40
            dw        280,260,300,328,360,370
            dw        360,320,340,360,280
draw        ends
;
;               stack
;
stack       segment  stack
            db        256 dup(?)
s_data      equ       $
stack       ends
            end       go
```

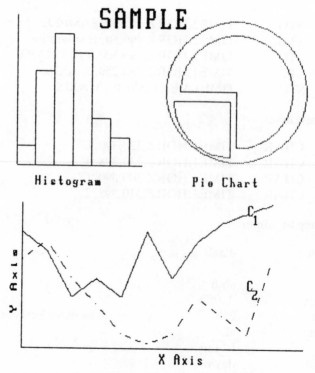

18.2 Screen dump on dot matrix printer.

APPENDIX A

Summary of 8086/8088 Instructions

The mnemonics are listed alphabetically with their full names.

Mnemonic	Description	Reference
AAA	ASCII adjust for addition	—
AAD	ASCII adjust for division	—
AAM	ASCII adjust for multiplication	—
AAS	ASCII adjust for subtraction	—
ADC	Add with carry	56
ADD	Add	54
AND	And	63
CALL	Procedure call	107
CBW	Convert byte to word	59
CLC	Clear carry flag	79
CLD	Clear direction flag	98
CLI	Clear interrupt flag	123
CMC	Complement carry flag	79
CMP	Compare	76
CMPS	Compare byte or word (of string)	97
CMPSB	Compare byte string	97
CMPSW	Compare word string	97
CWD	Convert word to double word	59
DAA	Decimal adjust for addition	—
DAS	Decimal adjust for subtraction	—
DEC	Decrement	56
DIV	Divide	59
ESC	Escape	—
HLT	Halt	—
IDIV	Integer divide	59
IMUL	Integer multiply	58

Mnemonic	Description	Reference
IN	Input byte or word	120
INC	Increment	56
INT	Interrupt	122
INTO	Interrupt on overflow	122
IRET	Interrupt return	122
JA	Jump on above	77
JAE	Jump on above or equal	77
JB	Jump on below	77
JBE	Jump on below or equal	77
JC	Jump on carry	77
JCXZ	Jump on cx zero	77
JE	Jump on equal	77
JG	Jump on greater	77
JGE	Jump on greater or equal	77
JL	Jump on less than	77
JLE	Jump on less than or equal	77
JMP	Jump unconditional	72
JNA	Jump on not above	77
JNAE	Jump on not above or equal	79
JNB	Jump on not below	79
JNBE	Jump on not below or equal	79
JNC	Jump on no carry	79
JNE	Jump on not equal	79
JNG	Jump on not greater	79
JNGE	Jump on not greater or equal	79
JNL	Jump on not less than	79
JNLE	Jump on not less than or equal	79
JNO	Jump on not overflow	79
JNP	Jump on not parity	79
JNS	Jump on not sign	79
JNZ	Jump on not zero	79
JO	Jump on overflow	79
JP	Jump on parity	79
JPE	Jump on parity even	79
JPO	Jump on parity odd	79
JS	Jump on sign	79
JZ	Jump on zero	79
LAHF	Load ah with flags	—
LDS	Load pointer into ds	50
LEA	Load effective address	50
LES	Load pointer into es	50
LOCK	Lock bus	—

Mnemonic	Description	Reference
LODS	Load byte or word (of string)	97
LODSB	Load byte (string)	97
LODSW	Load word (string)	97
LOOP	Loop until cx equal zero	86
LOOPE	Loop while equal	86
LOOPNE	Loop while not equal	86
LOOPNZ	Loop while not zero	86
LOOPZ	Loop while zero	86
MOV	Move	40
MOVS	Move byte or word (string)	97
MOVSB	Move byte (string)	97
MOVSW	Move word (string)	97
MUL	Multiply	58
NEG	Negate	56
NOP	No operation	—
NOT	Not	65
OR	Or	64
OUT	Output byte or word	121
POP	Pop	109
POPF	Pop flags	109
PUSH	Push	109
PUSHF	Push flags	109
RCL	Rotate through carry left	67
RCR	Rotate through carry right	67
REP	Repeat Prefix	100
RET	Return from procedures	107
ROL	Rotate left	66
ROR	Rotate right	67
SAHF	Store ah into flags	—
SAL	Shift arithmetic left	65
SAR	Shift arithmetic right	66
SBB	Subtract with borrow	56
SCAS	Scan byte or word (of string)	97
SCASB	Scan byte (string)	97
SCASW	Scan word (string)	97
SHL	Shift left	65
SHR	Shift right	66
STC	Set carry flag	79
STD	Set direction flag	98
STI	Set interrupt flag	123
STOS	Store byte or word (of string)	97
STOSB	Store byte (string)	97

Mnemonic	Description	Reference
STOSW	Store word (string)	97
SUB	Subtract	54
TEST	Test	77
WAIT	Wait	—
XCHG	Exchange	49
XLAT	Translate	102
XOR	Exclusive or	64

APPENDIX B

Listing of STDIO. ASM

COMMON INPUT/OUTPUT PROCEDURES

1.	PUTC	;output character
2.	PLINE	;output newline
3.	PLINES	;output n newlines
4.	PSTG	;output string of char terminated by a ;null character
5.	PCOUNT	;output string of char with count in cx
6.	PNUM	;output a signed number in decimal
7.	PNUMH	;output an unsigned number in hex.
8.	PASCII	;output in ASCII or '.'
9.	CLR	;clear screen, cursor 'home'
10.	GETC	;read character
11.	GNUM	;read signed decimal

86stdio.asm

```
;
;               this module defines a library of I/0 routines
;

                public    putc      ;screen display char in ax
                public    pline     ;screen display CR-LF
                public    plines    ;screen display no of CR-LF
                                    ;indicated by cx
                public    pstg      ;screen display string of char
                                    ;terminated by null
                public    pcount    ;display string with cx char
                public    pnum      ;screen display 16 bit signed dec
                public    pnumh     ;screen display 16 bit in hex
                public    pascii    ;screen display ascii or '.'
;
                public    getc      ;await a char from keyboard
```

```
            public     gnum            ;await a no from keyboard
                                       ;and translate to ascii
;
            public     clr             ;clear screen
            public     exit            ;ctrl C int
;
ESC         equ        27              ;ascii equivalent of esc
CR          equ        0dh
LF          equ        0ah
stdio       segment                    ;beginning of segment stdio
            assume cs:stdio            ;code segment used is stdio
;
putc        proc       far             ;define procedure
;
;           ENTRY:  char to be output in ax
;           EXIT:  output a byte
;           OTHER ROUTINES CALLED: system call: fn 2
;
            push       ax              ;save
            push       bx              ;       all the
            push       cx              ;              registers
            push       dx              ;                   on stack
;
            mov        dl,al           ;char to be output in dl
            mov        ah,2            ;msdos id for keyboard o/p → ah
            int        21h             ;msdos entry point
;
;           put a delay in, needed otherwise the screen cannot
;           handle the output
;
;           the delay loop
;
            mov        cx,0fh          ;count used for delay loop → cx
delay:      push       cx              ;save count on stack
            mov        cx,0ffh         ;count used for inner loop → cx
dely2:      nop                        ;instruction for delays
            loop       dely2           ;dec cx and loop till cx = 0
            pop        cx              ;restore loop count from stack
            loop       delay           ;dec cx and loop till cx = 0
;
;           return control to calling routine and restore regs
;
            pop        dx              ;restore
            pop        cx              ;       all the
            pop        bx              ;              registers
```

```
                 pop      ax             ;            from stack
                 ret                     ;exit to calling routine
    ;
    putc         endp                    ;end of this procedure
    ;
    pline        proc     far            ;beginning of procedure pline
    ;            ENTRY:   nothing
    ;            EXIT:    nothing
    ;            OTHER ROUTINES CALLED: putc
    ;
                 push     ax             ;save
                 push     bx             ;       all the
                 push     cx             ;             registers
                 push     dx             ;                   on stack
    ;
                 mov      al,CR          ;ascii value of carriage return
                 call     far ptr putc   ;display char in al
                 mov      al,LF          ;ascii value of linefeed → al
                 call     far ptr putc   ;display char in al
    ;
                 pop      dx             ;restore
                 pop      cx             ;       all the
                 pop      bx             ;             registers
                 pop      ax             ;                   from stack
                 ret                     ;exit to calling routine
    pline        endp                    ;end of this procedure
    ;
    plines       proc     far
    ;
    ;            ENTRY:   no of carriage return, line feed to be output
    ;                     in cx
    ;            EXIT:    output carriage return, line feed equivalent
    ;                     to the no in cx
    :            OTHER ROUTINES CALLED:  pline
    ;
                 push     ax             ;save
                 push     bx             ;       all the
                 push     cx             ;             registers
                 push     dx             ;                   on stack
    ;
    nlis:        call     far ptr pline  ;display a CR-LF
                 loop     nlis           ;cont till count in cx = 0
    ;
                 pop      dx             ;restore
```

```
                pop       cx          ;          all the
                pop       bx          ;                 registers
                pop       ax          ;                      on stack
                ret                   ;exit to calling routine
plines          endp                  ;end of this procedure
;
pstg            proc      far         ;beginning of proc pstg
;
;               ENTRY: ds:dx with the address of the message to be displayed
;               EXIT:     screen display string terminated by a null char
;
;               OTHER ROUTINES CALLED:  putc
;
                push      ax          ;save
                push      bx          ;          all the
                push      cx          ;                 registers
                push      dx          ;                      on stack
;
                mov       bx,dx       ;dx → base register
nstg:           mov       al,[bx]     ;content addressed by bx → al
                cmp       al,0        ;is it a null char
                jz        lstg        ;jump if it is
;
                call      far ptr putc ;display the char in al
                inc       bx          ;increment bx to ptr to next char
                jmp       nstg        ;jump to cont fetch chars
;
lstg:           pop       dx          ;restore
                pop       cx          ;          all the
                pop       bx          ;                 registers
                pop       ax          ;                      from stack
;
                ret                   ;exit to calling routine
pstg            endp                  ;end of this procedure
;


;
pcount          proc      far         ;beginning of procedure pcount
;
;               ENTRY:  ds:dx        address of 1st byte
;                       cx           number of bytes
;
;               EXIT:    display a string of char with no of char
;                             in cx count
;               OTHER ROUTINES CALLED: putc
;
```

```
        push     ax              ;save
        push     bx              ;     all the
        push     cx              ;          registers
        push     dx              ;               on stack
;
        mov      bx,dx           ;dx → base reg
ncnt:   mov      al,[bx]         ;content of loc addressed by bx
        call     far ptr putc    ;display al
        inc      bx              ;increment bx to point to next ch
        loop     ncnt            ;cont till count register is zero
;
        pop      dx              ;restore
        pop      cx              ;     all
        pop      bx              ;          the registers
        pop      ax              ;               from stack
        ret                      ;exit to calling routine
pcount  endp                     ;end of this routine
;


;
pnum    proc far                 ;define a procedure
;
;       pnum
;       ENTRY   ax = integer
;       EXIT    output the ascii equivalent of the binary value
;               in ax
;       OTHER ROUTINES CALLED:   putc
;
        push     ax              ;save
        push     bx              ;     all
        push     cx              ;          registers
        push     dx              ;               on stack
;
;       check if the number is positive
;
        mov      cx,0            ;clear digit count i.e. cx
        cmp      ax,0            ;cmp ax with immediate data '0'
        jge      ndigit          ;jump if ax → 0
;
;       the number is negative, output − sign
;
        push     ax              ;save the number on stack
        mov      al,'−'          ;'−' → al
        call     far ptr putc    ;o/p the char'−'
        pop      ax              ;retrieve the number from stack
```

```
          neg        ax                 ;negate the number
;
;          number now all positive
;
ndigit:   cwd                           ;convert ax to double word
          mov        bx,10              ;immediate date 10→ bx
          div        bx                 ;ax:ax/10
;
          push       dx                 ;save the remainder on stack
          inc        cx                 ;increment digit count
          cmp        ax,0               ;is quot = 0
          jnz        ndigit             ;jump if <> 0
;
nout:     pop        ax                 ;retrieve remainder from stack
          and        al,0fh             ;mask off the sign indications
          add        al,30h             ;convert to ascii
;
;          output a byte
;
          call       far ptr putc       ;o/p the ascii char
          loop       nout               ;cont to convert next number
;
;          restore
;
          pop        dx                 ;restore
          pop        cx                 ;       all
          pop        bx                 ;            the
          pop        ax                 ;                registers
          ret                           ;exit to calling routine
pnum      endp                          ;end of this procedure
;


;
pnumh     proc       far                ;beginning of procedure far
;
;          ENTRY   ax – 16 bit data
;          EXIT    16 bit in hex
;          OTHER ROUTINES CALLED: pnib
          push       ax                 ;save
          push       bx                 ;        all
          push       cx                 ;            the
          push       dx                 ;                registers
;
          mov        cl,12              ;12 → cl
nib2:     push       ax                 ;save ax on stack
```

```
        sar     ax,cl           ;shift right for paces in cl
        call    pnib            ;o/p ax in ascii
        sub     cl,4            ;update shift to be shifted
        cmp     cl,−4           ;cmp cl with −4
        pop     ax              ;restore ax from stack
        jnz     nib2            ;jump if cl <> −4
;
;       restore
;

        pop     dx              ;restore
        pop     cx              ;       all
        pop     bx              ;               registers
        pop     ax              ;                       from stack
        ret                     ;exit
pnumh   endp                    ;end of this procedure pnumh
;
pnib    proc    near            ;beginning of procedure pnib
;
;       ENTRY:  char in al
;       EXIT:   output lower 4 bit in hex
;       OTHER ROUTINES CALLED: none
        and     al,0fh          ;mask off the top 4 bits
;
;       translate to ascii and if the nibble is greater than 9
;       replace by a–f
;
        add     al,'0'          ;translate to ascii, add 30
        cmp     al,3ah          ;cmp al with ascii
        jl      ph3             ;<3ah means less than 9
;
        add     al,07           ;translate to a–f
ph3:    call    far ptr putc    ;o/p the char in ax
        ret                     ;exit to calling routine
pnib    endp                    ;end of this procedure
;


;
pascii  proc    far
;
;       ENTRY: al − char
;       EXIT: output on ASCII char or '.'
;       OTHER ROUTINES CALLED: putc
;
```

```
                push       ax              ;save
                push       bx              ;          all
                push       cx              ;                registers
                push       dx              ;                      on stack
;
                cmp        al,7fh          ;compare al with last ascii i.e.7fh
                jge        l__pasc1        ;jump if greater than 7fh
                cmp        al,20h          ;compare al with first printable
                jge        l__pasc2        ;char and jump if greater than
;
l__pasc1:       mov        al,'.'          ;replace al with '.'
l__pasc2:       call       far ptr putc    ;output the char
;
                pop        dx              ;restore
                pop        cx              ;       all
                pop        bx              ;             the registers
                pop        ax              ;                   from stack
                ret                        ;exit to calling routine
pascii          endp                       ;end of this procedure
;

;
getc            proc       far             ;beginning of this procedure getc
;
;       ENTRY: nothing
;       EXIT:    await a char at the keyboard
;       OTHER ROUTINE CALLED: system call : fn 1.b
;
                mov        ah,1            ;msdos id for keyboard input
                int        21h             ;msdos entry point
                ret                        ;return to calling routine
getc            endp                       ;end of this procedure
;
gnum            proc       far             ;beginning of this procedure gnum
;
;       ENTRY: nothing
;       EXIT:    read num from console and convert to non-ascii no
;                ax = binary equivalent of keyboard input
;       OTHER ROUTINES CALLED: putc
;                              system call : fn 6.
;
;
                push       bx              ;save
                push       cx              ;        registers
```

```
        push    dx            ;             on stack
;
;       initialize the conversion factors
;
        mov     dh,0          ;default sign to +ve
        mov     bx,10         ;decimal conversion constant
        mov     cx,0          ;0 → result register
;
;       await a keyboard input
;
rd1:    mov     ah,6          ;msdos id for keyboard input
        mov     dl,0ffh       ;direct input
        int     21h           ;msdos entry point
;
        cmp     al,0          ;cmp al with 0
        jz      rd1           ;if = 0 jump to rd1
;
;       check if the keyboard input char = ctrl c
;                                           new line
;
        cmp     al,3          ;cmp keyboard i/p with ctrl c
        jnz     rd2           ;if no, jump
        call    far ptr exit  ;exit to msdos
;
rd2:    cmp     al,CR         ;comp keyboard i/p with CR
        jz      rddone        ;if yes, jump to rddone
;
;       check for sign and validate for numeric
;
        cmp     al,'–'        ;cmp keyboard i/p with '–'
        jnz     vdigit        ;jump if not, i.e. +ve no
;
        mov     dh,0ffh       ;set sign flag
        call    far ptr putc  ;display the '–' sign
        jmp     rd1           ;read next digit
;
vdigit: cmp     al,'0'        ;cmp keyboard i/o with ascii 0
        jb      rd1           ;if less ignore
;
        cmp     al,'9'        ;cmp keyboard i/o with ascii 9
        jg      rd1           ;if greater, ignore
;
        call    putc          ;echo the keyboard i/o
;
        sub     al,'0'        ;convert to binary from ascii
```

```
        cbw                         ;convert to 16 bit in ax
        push    dx                  ;save the sign identifier
        push    ax                  ;save the keyboard i/p
;
        mov     ax,cx               ;cx → ax
        mul     bx                  ;multiply by conversion constant
        pop     cx                  ;restore keyboard i/p → cx
        pop     dx                  ;restore sign id → dx
;
        add     ax,cx               ;converted no → ax
        mov     cx,ax               ;result → count register
        jmp     rd1                 ;jump to wait for next i/p
;
;       end of i/p,hence the number according to the sign
;
rddone: cmp     dh,0                ;check if the sign is 0
        jz      nochg               ;jump if yes
        neg     cx                  ;else complement the no
;
nochg:  mov     ax,cx               ;the convert no. → ax
        call    far ptr pline       ;output a cr,lf
;
        pop     dx                  ;restore
        pop     cx                  ;        registers
        pop     bx                  ;               from stack
        ret                         ;return to calling routine
gnum    endp                        ;end of this procedure
;
;       clear screen
;
clr     proc    far
;
;       ENTRY:  nothing
;       EXIT:   nothing
;       FUNCTION: clear screen
;
        push    ax                  ;save ax register
;
;       send clear screen command i.e. ESC 'E'
;
        mov     al,ESC              ;ascii equivalent of ESC → al
        call    far ptr putc        ;o/p ESC
        mov     al,'E'              ;'E' → al
        call    far ptr putc        ;o/p 'E'
        pop     ax                  ;restore ax from stack
```

```
        ret            ;restore to calling routine
clr     endp           ;end of this procedure
;
;       return control to msdos i.e. a warm boot
;
exit    proc  far      ;beginning of procedure exit
        int   23h      ;msdos entry for warm boot
exit    endp           ;end of this procedure
;
stdio   ends           ;end of this segment
```

APPENDIX C

Listing of COMMS Programs

```
86send.asm
;
;              MSDOS    comms    program
;
;
;              a program to send characters via port b
;
code           segment    public
               assume cs:code,ds:code,ss:stack
;
;              define procedures in comm.asm
;
               extrn      baud:near          ;set baud rate to be 4800
               extrn      send:near          ;send a char to port b
               extrn      receive:near       ;receive a char from port b
               extrn      shocrt:near        ;o/p message on screen
               extrn      purgeline:near     ;clear port b
;
;              defined procedures in stdio
;
               extrn      pcount:far         ;o/p char string length in cx
               extrn      pnum:far           ;output number
               extrn      pstg:far           ;output a char string
               extrn      putc:far           ;output a char
               extrn      pline:far          ;o/p a line on screen
               extrn      exit:far           ;exit to msdos
;
;              define symbols
;
DOS                       equ    21h         ;interrupt for msdos functions
```

```
READCON        equ    1            ;msdos function id,read console
OPENFL         equ    0fh          ;                 ,open file
SETDMA         equ    1ah          ;                 ,set dma
READFL         equ    14h          ;                 ,read file
PARSEFL        equ    29h          ;                 ,setfile name
;
SOH            equ    1            ;ascii equivalent for SOH
EOT            equ    4            ;                    EOT
ACK            equ    6            ;                    ACK
BELL           equ    7            ;                    BELL
NAK            equ    21           ;                    ACK
ERRORMAX       equ    10           ;maximum no of error allowed
RETRYMAX       equ    10           ;maximum no of retrys
;
EOF            equ    -1           ;end of file id in disk read
SECSIZE        equ    128          ;size of sector
NSECT          equ    8            ;no of sectors in ram
BUFSIZ         equ    (nsect * secsize + 7)    ;buffer size
;
;          define structure
;
;          fcb of the file to be sent
;
fcb            struc               ;name of structure is fcb
drive          db     0            ;name of drive of the file
filename       db     '    '       ;name of file
ftype          db     '   '        ;file type
fext           dw     0            ;file extent
frecord        dw     128          ;size of file record
fsize          dd     0            ;no of records in the file
fdate          dw     0            ;last accessed date
ftime          dw     0            ;last accessed time
fresv          db     8 dup (?)    ;reserve 8 bytes for msdos
fcr            db     0            ;current record
frand          dd     0            ;random record number
fcb            ends                ;end of this structure definition
;
;          macro definitions
;
;
;          define macro outnum
;
M_OUTNUM       macro  arg1         ;macro m outnum
               mov    ax,arg1      ;first argument → ax
               call   pnum         ;o/p ax as number
```

```
                 endm                              ;end of this macro
;
M__OUTCH         macro    arg1                     ;macro m outch
                 mov      al,arg1                  ;first argument → al
                 call     putc                     ;o/p the char in al
                 endm                              ;end of this macro
;
M__OUTSTG        macro    stg                      ;macro m outstg
                 local    message,l__out           ;local labels used
                 jmp      l__out                   ;jump to first instruction
message          db       '&stg',0                 ;data area used
l__out:          mov      dx,offset message        ;addr of o/p mess → dx
                 call     pstg                     ;o/p string
                 endm                              ;end of this macro
;
M__SHOCRT        macro    arg1,arg2,arg3           ;macro m shocrt
                 push     arg3                     ;save third arg on stack
                 push     arg2                     ;save second arg on stack
                 push     arg1                     ;save first arg on stack
                 call     shocrt                   ;o/p string
                 endm                              ;end of this macro
;
;         main module begin from loc go
;
;         init segment registers
;
go:              mov      ax,code                  ;data segment is set
                 mov      ds,ax                    ;as code
                 mov      ax,stack                 ;stack segment is set
                 mov      ss,ax                    ;as stack
                 mov      sp,offset s__data        ;set stack pointer
;
;         output signon message
;
          M__OUTSTG ─ ⟨BCY Copyright (C) 1983⟩
                 call     pline                    ;o/p a blank line
                 call     pline                    ;o/p a blank line
                 call     baud                     ;set to 4800 baud
;
;         copy filename from command line
;
                 les      di,fcbptr                ;fcbptr → es & di
                 lds      si,comptr                ;comptr → ds & si
                 mov      ah,PARSEFL               ;id for name file function
                 mov      al,0                     ;id for 1 name in command line
```

```
                int       DOS                    ;entry to msdos
        ;
        ;       display the name of the file to be transferred
        ;
                mov       ax,code                ;reset ds
                mov       ds,ax                  ;   into code segment
        ;
                M__OUTSTG ⟨file⟩                  ;o/p the chars file
                mov       dx,offset sfcb.filename ;addr of filename → dx
                mov       cx,11                  ;length of o/p chars → cx = 11
                call      pcount                 ;o/p name of the file
        ;
        ;       open file
        ;
l__op6:         mov       ah,OPENFL              ;id for open file fn > ah
                mov       dx,offset sfcb         ;file fcb → dx
                int       DOS                    ;enter into msdos
                inc       al                     ;increment al
                jnz       l__op8                 ;jmp if no error
        ;
        ;       ERROR, file cannot be opened fatal error
        ;
                M__OUTSTG ⟨not found⟩             ;o/p not found
                M__OUTCH   BELL                  ;sound the bell
                call      exit                   ;return control to msdos
        ;
        ;       display file size in sectors
        ;
l__op8:         M__OUTSTG ⟨is⟩                    ;o/p the chars is
                mov       bx,offset sfcb.fsize   ;addr of fcb → bx
                mov       ax,[bx]                ;file size returned by
                inc       bx                     ;the open function as
                inc       bx                     ;the second byte in fcb
        ;
                mov       dx,[bx]                ;double word fsize in bytes
                mov       bx,128                 ;size of sector → bx
                div       bx                     ;dx / bx
                cmp       dx,0                   ;check if remainder is zero
                jz        los__2                 ;no jump
                inc       ax                     ;yes, extra sector
        ;
los__2:         call      pnum                   ;o/p the number of sectors
                M__OUTSTG ⟨sectors long.⟩         ;o/p chars sectors long
                call      pline                  ;o/p a blank line
        ;
```

```
;           initialize various parameters
;
los4:       mov     ax,0e004h              ;top 16 bit of port number
            mov     es,ax                  ;→ es
;
            call    purgeline              ;clear the port
            sub     ax,ax                  ;set 0 → ax
            mov     attempts,ax            ;attempts = 0
            mov     toterr,ax              ;toterr = 0
            M_SHOCRT   zero,zero,zero      ;o/p three zeros
;
;           attempt to locate the remote computer by waiting for
;           an NAK
;           give up after ten seconds
;
lm__40:     mov     bx,10                  ;no of secs → bx
            call    receive                ;char at port b → al
            cmp     al,NAK                 ;check if it is a nak
            jnz     lm__60                 ;if not jump
            jmp     lm__100                ;else jump
;
lm__60:     cmp     attempts,8             ;check if attempts = 8
            jz      lm__80                 ;if yes jump
            inc     attempts               ;increment attempts
            M_SHOCRT   zero,attempts,zero  ;o/p no of attempts
            jmp     short   lm__40         ;jump
;
;           ERROR,  time allowed expired
;                   enquire if the user like to continue or abort
;
lm__80:     call    pline                  ;o/p a blank line
            M_OUTSTG ⟨Timeout awaiting initial NAK⟩
                                           ;o/p error message
            call    pline                  ;o/p a blank line
            M_OUTSTG ⟨Type any key to retry, or ctrl c to abort⟩
            call    pline                  ;o/p a blank line
            mov     ah,READCON             ;id for msdos fn read keyboard
            int     DOS                    ;msdos entry point
            jmp     los4                   ;jump
;
;           an ack is received, send first sector
;
lm__100:    sub     ax,ax                  ;reset
```

```
        mov     attempts,ax         ;           attempts
        inc     ax                  ;increment ax
        mov     sectnum,ax          ;sectnum = 1
;
;       main loop in sending data from specified file
;
lm__106: call   read                ;read next eight sectors
        cmp     ax,EOF              ;check if any read error
        jnz     lm__108             ;jump if no error
;
;       ERROR, disk read error encountered, display error message
;
        call    pline               ;o/p a blank line
        M__OUTSTG  ⟨file read error.⟩  ;o/p error message
        call    pline               ;o/p a blank line
        jmp     lm__300             ;jmp to end of file handler
;
;       successful read, hence send the sector
;
lm__108: cmp    ax,0                ;check the record number
        jnz     lm__120             ;if ⟨⟩ 0 read next sector
        jmp     lm__300             ;jump to end of file handler
;
;       set displays on screen
;
lm__120: mov    sectors,ax          ;sector = read(fd,buffer,8)
        mov     bx,0                ;init buffer ptr → bx
lm__140: mov    attempts, 0         ;init attempts = 0
lm__160: mov    si,bx               ;init index ptr
        M__SHOCRT   sectnum,attempts,toterr   ;o/p parameters
;
;       set up message header
;
        mov     al,SOH              ;send SOH
        call    send
        mov     ax,sectnum          ;send sector number
        call    send
        mov     ax,sectnum          ;send –(sector number)
        neg     ax
        dec     ax
        call    send
;
        sub     dh,dh               ;init checksum = 0
        mov     cx,SECSIZE          ;sector size → cx = 128
;
```

```
;           send byte and byte and update checksum continuously
;           checksum = (checksum + data) and 0ffh
;
lm__200:    mov     al,sbuf[si]              ;next byte of data → al
            add     dh,al                    ;update checksum
            call    send                     ;send(data)
            inc     si                       ;increment buffer ptr
            loop    lm__200                  ;repeat till 128 bytes sent
;
            mov     al,dh                    ;checksum → al
            call    send                     ;send(checksum)
            call    purgeline                ;clear port
;
            inc     attempts                 ;increment attempts
            inc     toterr                   ;increment toterr
;
;           a complete sector is sent
;           wait for an ack before continue
;
            push    bx                       ;save buffer ptr on stack
            mov     bx,10                    ;set wait time = 10 sec
            call    receive                  ;scan port b
            pop     bx                       ;restore buffer ptr
            cmp     al,ACK                   ;check if ACK is received
            jz      lm__220                  ;yes, jump
;
            cmp     attempts,RETRYMAX        ;check if tried enough
            jnz     lm__160                  ;no try again
            jmp     lm__400
;
;           set parameters for sending next sector
;
lm__220:    add     bx,SECSIZE               ;update buffer ptr
            inc     sectnum                  ;increment sector no
            dec     toterr                   ;decrement toterr
            dec     sectors                  ;update remaining sectors
            jnz     lm__140                  ;if not all sent, cont
            jmp     lm__106                  ;else start on next batch
;
;           end of file transfer
;           send EOT, wait for an ACK for 10 retrys
;           if fail, display error message
;
lm__300:    mov     attempts,0               ;0 → attempts
lm__320:    mov     al,EOT                   ;ascii EOT → al
```

```
        call      send                    ;send EOT
        call      purgeline               ;clear port
;
        inc       attempts                ;increment attempts
        cmp       attempts, RETRYMAX      ;check if tried enough
        jz        lm__340                 ;if yes, jump
;
        mov       bx,10                   ;no of seconds → bx = 10
        call      receive                 ;read port b
        cmp       al,ACK                  ;check if char at b = ACK
        jnz       lm__320                 ;try again
;
;       ACK is received, display message and exit to msdos
;
        call      pline                   ;o/p a blank line
        M_OUTSTG  (Done – return to operating system)   ;o/p mess
        jmp       short lm__600           ;exit to msdos
;
;       ERROR, no ACK, hence display error message
;
lm__340: call     pline                   ;display blank line
        M_OUTSTG  (No ACK on end__of__file,aborting)  ;o/p error
        M_OUTCH   BELL                    ;sound the bell
        jmp       short lm__600           ;exit to msdos
;
;       ERROR, no ACK on end of sector, hence display error mess
;
lm__400: call     pline                   ;display blank line
        M_OUTSTG  (No ACK on sector, aborting)   ;o/p error
        M_OUTCH   BELL                    ;sound the bell
lm__600: call     exit                    ;exit to msdos
;*****************************************************************
;
;       define    proc  read
;
read     proc     near
;
;       set DMA address
;
        mov       dx,offset sbuf          ;start of buffer → dx
        mov       i__ptr,dx               ;→ current dma buffer
        mov       cx,8                    ;no of sector → cx = 8
;
lrd__0: mov       dx,i__ptr               ;current dma buffer → dx
        mov       ah,setdma               ;id for msdos fn set dma
```

```
                int       DOS                     ;enter to msdos
;
;               read a sector
;
                mov       ah,readfl               ;id for msdosfnreadfile
                mov       dx,offset sfcb          ;fcb address → dx
                int       DOS                     ;enter to msdos
;
;               check if read error
;
                cmp       al,0                    ;check if al = 0
                jnz       lrd__chk                ;if not jump
;
                add       iptr,SECSIZE            ;next sector
                loop      lrd__0                  ;repeat till 8 sectors
                                                  ;are read
;
;               end of file reached,
;               return with no of remaining sectors in ax
;
lrd__eof:       mov       ax,8                    ;
                sub       ax,cx                   ;no of sector read
                ret                               ;exit to calling routine
;
lrd__chk:       cmp       al,1                    ;check if end of file
                jz        lrd__eof                ;yes jump
;
                cmp       al,3                    ;check if partially filled
                jnz       lrd__err                ;if not jump
;
                dec       cx                      ;decrement sector count
                jmp       short lrd__eof          ;end of file reached jump
;
;               ERROR, return with EOF in ax
;
lrd__err:       mov       ax,EOF                  ;read err
                ret                               ;exit to msdos
;
i__ptr          dw        0                       ;current dma pointer
read            endp                              ;end of this procedure
;
;               global data area
;
sfcb            fcb       <,' ',' '>              ;
comptr          dd        02c00102h               ;command line ptr
```

```
fcbptr          dd          sfcb                        ;fcb ptr
zero            dw          0                           ;value zero
attempts        dw          0                           ;no of attempts
toterr          dw          0                           ;total number of error
sectors         dw          0                           ;sector count
sectnum         dw          0                           ;sector number
sbuf            db          BUFSIZ dup (?)              ;disk read buffer
;
code            ends                                    ;end of this segment
;
;
;               stack segment
;
stack           segment     stack                       ;start of stack segment
                db          256 dup(?)                  ;reserve 256 bytes for stack
sdata           equ         $                           ;stack pointer
stack           ends                                    ;end of stack segment
                end         go                          ;end of this program


;
;               MSDOS comms program
;
;
;               a program to RECEIVE characters via port b
;
code            segment     public
                assume cs:code,ds:code,ss:stack
;
;               define procedures in comm.asm
;
                extrn       baud:near                   ;set baud rate to be 4800
                extrn       send:near                   ;send a char to port b
                extrn       receive:near                ;receive a char from port b
                extrn       shocrt:near                 ;o/p message on screen
                extrn       purgeline:near              ;clear port b
;
;               defined procedures in stdio
;
                extrn       pcount:far                  ;o/p char string length in cx
                extrn       pnum:far                    ;output number
                extrn       pstg:far                    ;output a char string
                extrn       putc:far                    ;output a char
                extrn       pline:far                   ;o/p a line on screen
                extrn       exit:far                    ;exit to msdos
;
```

```
;               define symbols
;
DOS            equ     21h        ;interrupt for msdos functions
READCON        equ     1          ;msdos funtion id,read console
OPENFL         equ     0fh        ;              ,open file
CLOSEFL        equ     10h        ;              ,close file
WRITEFL        equ     15h        ;              ,write record
CREATFL        equ     16h        ;              ,create file
SETDMA         equ     1ah        ;              ,set dma
READFL         equ     14h        ;              ,read file
PARSEFL        equ     29h        ;              ,setfile name
;
;               define symbols
;
TRUE           equ     0          ;msdos id for true
FALSE          equ     -1         ;msdos id for false
TIMEOUT        equ     -1         ;msdos id for timeout
SOH            equ     1          ;ascii equivalent for SOH
EOT            equ     4          ;              EOT
ACK            equ     6          ;              ACK
NAK            equ     21         ;              ACK
ERRORMAX       equ     10         ;maximum no of error allowed
RETRYMAX       equ     10         ;maximum no of retrys
;
EOF            equ     -1         ;end of file id in disk read
SECSIZE        equ     128        ;size of sector
NSECT          equ     8          ;no of sectors in ram
BUFSIZ         equ     (nsect * secsize + 7)   ;buffer size
;
;
;               define structure
;               fcb of the file to be sent
;
fcb            struc              ;name of structure is fcb
drive          db      0          ;name of drive of the file
filename       db      '          ';name of file
ftype          db      '          ;file type
fext           dw      0          ;file extent
frecord        dw      128        ;size of file record
fsize          dd      0          ;no of records in the file
fdate          dw      0          ;last accessed date
ftime          dw      0          ;last accessed time
fresv          db      8 dup (?)  ;reserve 8 bytes for msdos
```

```
fcr         db        0                    ;current record
frand       dd        0                    ;random record number
fcb         ends                           ;end of this structure definition
;
;
;           macro definitions
;

M__OUTNUM   macro     arg1                 ;macro m outnum
            mov       ax,arg1              ;first argument → ax
            call      pnum                 ;o/p ax as number
            endm                           ;end of this macro

;
M__OUTCH    macro     arg1                 ;macro m outch
            mov       al,arg1              ;first argument → al
            call      putc                 ;o/p the char in al
            endm                           ;end of this macro

;
M__OUTSTG   macro     stg                  ;macro m outstg
            local     message,l__out       ;local labels used
            jmp       l__out               ;jump to first instruction
message     db        '&stg',0             ;data area used
l__out:     mov       dx,offset message    addr of o/p mess → dx
            call      pstg                 ;o/p string
            endm                           ;end of this macro

;
M__SCHOCRT  macro     arg1,arg2,arg3       ;macro m shocrt
            push      arg3                 ;save third arg on stack
            push      arg2                 ;save second arg on stack
            push      arg1                 ;save first arg on stack
            call      shocrt               ;o/p string
            endm                           ;end of this macro


;
;
;
;           main module begin from loc go
;
;           init segment registers
;
;
go:         mov       ax,code              ;data segment is set
            mov       ds,ax                ;as code
            mov       ax,stack             ;stack segment is set
            mov       ss,ax                ;as stack
```

```
                mov        sp,offset s__data          ;set stack pointer
;
;               output signon message
;
                m__OUTSTG ⟨BCY Copyright (C) 1983⟩
                call       pline                      ;o/p a blank line
                call       pline                      ;o/p a blank line
                call       baud                       ;set to 1200 baud
;
;               copy filename from command line
;
                les        di,fcbptr                  ;fcbptr → es & di
                lds        si,comptr                  ;comptr → ds & si
                mov        ah,PARSEFL                 ;id for name file function
                mov        al,0                       ;id for 1 name in command line
                int        DOS                        ;entry to msdos
;
;               reset data segment
;
                mov        ax,code                    ;reset ds
                mov        ds,ax                      ;   into code segment
;
;               open file
;
1__op2:         mov        ah,OPENFL                  ;id for msdos fn openfile → ah
                mov        dx,offset sfcb             ;file fcb → dx
                int        DOS                        ;msdos entry point
                inc        al                         ;check if file already exists
                jz         1__op4                     ;jump if not exists
;
;               no file open error, hence file already exists
;
                M__OUTSTG ⟨file⟩                      ;o/p char file
                mov        dx,offset sfcb,filename    ;name of file → dx
                mov        cx,11                      ;no of chars to o/p → cx
                call       pcount                     ;o/p chars
                M__OUTSTG ⟨already exist.⟩            ;o/p already exist
                call       exit                       ;return to msdos
;
;               file open error, hence create file
;
1__op4:         mov        ah,CREATFL                 ;msdos fn id create file → ah
                mov        dx,offset sfcb             ;file fcb to create → dx
                int        DOS                        ;msdos entry point
                inc        al                         ;check for disk error
```

```
        jnz     l__op8                  ;jump if no error
;
;               ERROR, fatal, create error
;
                M__OUTSTG  ⟨  cannot create  ⟩
;o/p error message
        mov     dx,offset sfcb.filename   ;name of file → dx
        mov     cx,11                   ;no of char → cx
        call    pcount                  ;o/p filename
        call    exit                    ;return to msdos
;
;               file created, ready to receive data from port
;
l__op8: M__OUTSTG ⟨Ready to receive⟩;o/p message
        mov     dx,offset sfcb.filename;filename → dx
        mov     cx,11                   ;length of filename → cx
        call    pcount                  ;o/p filename
        call    pline                   ;o/p a blank line
;
;               main loop in receiving data from port b
;
l__os4: mov     ax,0e004h               ;port address → ax
        mov     es,ax                   ; → es
;
;               initialization
;
        call    purgeline               ;clear port
        sub     ax,ax                   ;0 → ax
        mov     errors, ax              ;init errors = 0
        mov     toterr,ax               ;init toterr = 0
        mov     sectnum, ax             ;init sectnum = 0
        mov     bufctr,ax               ;init bufctr = 0
        M__SHOCRT   zero,zero,zero       ;o/p parameters
;
;               wait for SOH, EOT and check time expires
;
;
lm__100: mov    bx,10                   ;max. no of second allowed
        call    receive                 ;read from port
        cmp     al,SOH                  ;check if SOH is received
        jz      lm__140                 ;jump if yes
;
        cmp     al,EOT                  ;jump if EOT is received
        jnz     lm__120
        jmp     lm__420
```

```
;
lm__120:  cmp    al,TIMEOUT           ;if time has expired
          jnz    lm__100
          jmp    lm__360
;
;         got SOH, start receive data
;
lm__140:  mov    bx,1                 ;allow 1 sec for receive
          call   receive             ;read from port
          mov    byte ptr sectcurr,al ;al → current sector no
          mov    bx,1                 ;allow 1 sec for receive
          call   receive             ;read from port
          add    al,byte ptr sectcurr ;complement is received
          inc    al                  ;check for error
          jz     lm__160             ;no error jump
          jmp    lm__360             ;error, jump
;
;         check if the same sector is receiving
;
lm__160   mov    ax,sectnum          ;check next byte
          inc    ax
          cmp    al,byte ptr sectcurr
          jz     lm__180
;
          mov    ax,sectnum
          cmp    al,byte ptr sctnum  ;if (sectcurr = = sectnum)
          jz     lm__164
          jmp    lm__360             ;errorflag = TRUE
;
lm__164:  mov    bx,1
          call   receive             ;read from port
          cmp    al,TIMEOUT
          jnz    lm__164             ;loop till al <> TIMEOUT);
          mov    al,ACK
          jmp    lm__400             ;end of do loop
;
;         main loop in rec
;
lm__180:  mov    checksum,0          ;checksum = 0
          mov    si,bufctr           ;j = bufctr
          mov    cx,SECSIZE          ;loop count
lm__200:  push   cx
          mov    bx,1
          call   receive             ;receive from port
          add    checksum,al         ;checksum = (checksum + data) a
```

```
        mov     sbuf[si],al
        inc     si                      ;next byte
        pop     cx
        loop    lm__200
;
        mov     bx,1
        call    receive                 ;read from port
        cmp     checksum,al             ;is checksum = receive (1)?
        jz      lm__220
        jmp     lm__360                 ;errorflag = TRUE
;
lm__220: mov    errors,0
        mov     ax,sectcurr
        mov     sectnum,ax              ;sectnum = sectcurr
        add     bufctr,SECSIZE
        cmp     bufctr,SECSIZE * NSECT;total size
        jnz     lm__240
;
;       write whole buffer out
;
        mov     bufctr,0                ;bufctr = 0
        mov     cx,NSECT
        call    write                   ;disk write seq.
;
lm__240: M__SHOCRT   sectnum,errors, toterr
        mov     al,ACK
        call    send
        jmp     short lm__400
;
;       error flag == TRUE
;
lm__360: inc    errors
        cmp     sectnum,0
        jz      lm__380
        inc     toterr
lm__380: mov    bx,1
        call    receive                 ;read from port
        cmp     al,TIMEOUT
        jnz     lm__380                 ;loop till al <> (TIMEOUT);
;
        M__SHOCRT   sectnum,errors,toterr
        mov     al,NAK
        call    send
;
lm__400: cmp    errors,ERRORMAX
```

```
            jz          lm__460
            jmp         lm__100
;
;           done it at last
;
lm__420:    cmp         errors,ERRORMAX
            jz          lm__460
            mov         al,ACK
            call        send
            mov         ax,bufctr
            cwd
            mov         bx,SECSIZE
            div         bx
            cmp         dx,0
            jz          lm__440
            inc         ax
lm__440:    cmp         ax,0
            jz          lm__450             ;no more sectors
            mov         cx,ax
            call        write
;
;           close the file
;
lm__450:    mov         ah,CLOSFL           ;msdos id for close file
            mov         dx,offset sfcb      ;fcb add → dx
            int         dos                 ;msdos entry point
;
            call        pline               ;o/p a blank line
            M__OUTSTG   ⟨Done − return to operating system⟩
            jmp         short lm__600
;
            ;ERROR, fatal
;
lm__460:    call        pline               ;o/p a blank line
            M__OUTSTG ⟨Aborting⟩            ;o/p error message
lm__600:    call        exit                ;return to msdos
;***************************************************************************
;
;
;           define proc write
;
write       proc        near
;
;           set DMA address
;           entry cx − no. of sectors
;
            mov         dx,offset sbuf      ;beginning of buffer
```

```
            mov     i__ptr,dx                ;       → current ptr
;
lrd__0:     mov     dx,i__ptr                ;buffer ptr → dx
            mov     ah,SETDMA                ;msdos fn id for set dma
            int     DOS                      ;msdos entry point
;
;           write a sector
;
            mov     ah,WRITEFL               ;msdos fn id for write
            mov     dx,offset sfcb           ;fcb address
            int     DOS                      ;msdos entry point
;
;           check if read error
;
            cmp     al,0                     ;check al for disk error
            jnz     lrd__chk                 ;jump if error
            add     i__ptr,SECSIZE           ;increment buffer ptr
            loop    lrd__0                   ;repeat till cx = 0
            ret                              ;exit to calling routine
;
;           ERROR, fatal disk write error
;
lrd__chk:   M__OUTSTG ⟨disk write error⟩    ;o/p error message
            ret                              ;exit to calling routine
i__ptr      dw      0
write       endp
;
;           global data area
;
sfcb        fcb     ⟨,'     ',' ⟩            ;
comptr      dd      02c00102h                ;command line ptr
fcbptr      dd      sfcb                     ;fcb ptr
zero        dw      0                        ;value zero
attempts    dw      0                        ;no of attempts
toterr      dw      0                        ;total number of error
errors      dw      0                        ;no of errors
bufctr      dw      0                        ;buffer counter
sectors     dw      0                        ;sector count
sectnum     dw      0                        ;sector number
sbuf        db      BUFSIZ dup (?)           ;disk read buffer
;
code        ends                             ;end of this segment
;
;
;           stack   segment
;
stack       segment stack                    ;start of stack segment
```

```
                db      256 dup(?)              ;reserve 256 bytes for stack
s__data         equ     $                       ;stack pointer
stack           ends                            ;end of stack segment
                end     go                      ;end of this program
```

comm.asm
```
;
;               routines that are common to both 86rec and 86send program
;
;
CPUCLK          EQU     8                       ;clock rate in MHz
SPS             EQU     1500                    ;loops per second
TIMEOUT         EQU     -1
CR              EQU     0dh
PSTAT           EQU     3
PDATA           EQU     1
;
code            segment public
                assume cs:code,ds:code
;
include IO.MAC
;
                public  baud                    ;set baud rate
                public  send                    ;write to port
                public  receive                 ;read from port
                public  shocrt                  ;o/p mess on screen
                public  purgeline               ;clear port
;
;               extrn   pline:far               ;o/p a blank line
;
;               ACT Sirius comms procs
;
;               set baud rate for 2nd serial port to 1200
;
baud            proc    near
                mov     ax,0e002h
                mov     es,ax
;
                mov     byte ptr es:[PSTAT],54
                mov     byte ptr es:[PDATA],10h
                mov     byte ptr es:[PDATA],0
                ret
baud            endp
;
send            proc    near
```

```
;
;               on entry
;               es —      0e004h
;               al —      data
;
ls__noop:       mov       dl,es:[PSTAT]         ;read status byte
                and       dl,04                ;read ready bit
                jz        ls__noop             ;not ready
                mov       es:[PDATA],al        ;output char
                ret
send            endp
;
;               receive – read from port
;
receive         proc      near
;
;               receive
;
;               read char from port
;
;               on entry :-
;               reg bx    second
;                   es    0e004
;               return
;               al = data or
;                     TIMEOUT
;
                mov       cx,CPUCLK            ;outer loop count
lr__lpc:        push      cx
                mov       ax,SPS
                mul       bx
                mov       cx,ax               ;inner loop count
                                               (seccnt)
;
lr__rd:         mov       al,es:[PSTAT]
                and       al,01               ;read status
                jnz       lr__ok
;
                loop      lr__rd              ;inner loop with timeout
;
                pop       cx
                loop      lr__lpc             ;timeout on specified time
                mov       al,TIMEOUT
                ret
;
lr__ok:         pop       cx
```

```
                mov        al,es:[PDATA]            ;read data
                ret
receive         endp
;
shocrt          proc       near
;
;               shocrt
;
;               output message line on screen
;
;               on entry :-
;
;               sp+6       total count
;               sp+4       no of try
;               sp+2       sector no
;               sp         return address
;
;               define arguments on stacks
;
i__sec          equ        word ptr [bp+6]
i__try          equ        word ptr [bp+8]
i__tot          equ        word ptr [bp+10]
;
                push       bp
                push       ax
                mov        bp,sp                    ;bp points to current stack
;
                M__OUTSTG  ⟨Sending⟩
                M__OUTNUM  i__sec
;
                M__OUTSTG  ⟨try =⟩
                M__OUTNUM  i__try
;
                M__OUTSTG  ⟨errs =⟩
                M__OUTNUM  i__tot
                M__OUTCH   CR
;
                mov        ax,i__try
                and        ax,i__tot
                jz         lsh__skip
                call       pline
;
lsh__skip:      mov        sp,bp
                pop        ax
                pop        bp
```

```
            ret        6
;
shocrt      endp
;
purgeline   proc       near
;
;           clear  port
;
;           on entry
;           es         0e004h
;
lp__next:   mov        al,es:[PSTAT]
            and        al,01
            jz         lp__ret
            mov        al,es:[PDATA]
            jmp        short lp__next
lp__ret:    ret
purgeline              endp
            code       ends
            end
```

Index